BIG
BAD
BANKS

How greed and ego among big shots
in banking and government created
the crisis that wrecked our economy

BY C.R. 'RUSTY' CLOUTIER

First printing 2009

Library of Congress Catalog Card Number: 2009938644

ISBN: 978-0-615-31726-7

Published by Cloutier Publishing, LLC, Lafayette, La.

Book and jacket design by Robert S. Davis

Printed by Edward Brothers, Inc., Ann Arbor, Mich.

To my wife, Brenda

"I fell in love with two things in my life: my wife, Brenda, and the business of banking."

— Rusty Cloutier, March 2004

Contents

Introduction

THE VIEW FROM THE BAYOU

I've been a banker for just about all of my adult life. I learned banking from the ground up, starting as a fledgling teller in Morgan City, La. But even before I got that first banking job I knew that it was absolutely essential that any bank has to be trusted. I learned that lesson from my father, who was in high school in 1933 when one day the word spread that the local bank would be closed. He ran all the way to the bank to get the family's money out, but he was too late. The doors were padlocked and the money was gone. That, he told me, was the end of his dreams of college. Without a degree he wound up working on oil service industry boats along the Louisiana coast, a grueling and dangerous job.

Over time, though, my father became acquainted with some folks in Morgan City who had started a bank. They renewed his trust in bankers and he became convinced that the banking industry wasn't the root cause of his family losing its money. Rather, it was speculation and manipulation by Wall Street that led to the Depression. He also had faith that Washington had put in regulations that would prevent such actions from recurring. Even during the height of the Savings and Loan Crisis in the 1980s, when the government was closing savings institutions and banks right and left, he pointed out to me that thanks to federal deposit insurance, children weren't seeing their college money disappear. He sure wished there had been a Federal Deposit Insurance Corporation in 1933.

The way I learned it in Morgan City, banking should be an extremely simple business: take in money from depositors, lend it carefully to qualified borrowers, and make money on the difference between what you pay the depositors and what you charge the borrowers. Banks, out of necessity, should be conservative businesses as trust is — or was — the coin of their realm. When I became a loan officer, my manager drilled into me the Three Cs of Credit: capacity, character, and collateral. In other words, don't make a loan to someone who doesn't have the capacity to repay it or someone whose business dealings you know to be less than honorable. Even then, always have some collateral from your borrower in case your judgments about his capacity and character are wrong. Simple, isn't it?

But in the last 30 years banking became heedlessly lax and needlessly complex as ambitious executives, aided and abetted by regulators and elected officials, pushed their institutions to become bigger and more profitable, which is the same thing as riskier.

I understand the urge to become bigger. There are certain economies of scale available to bigger institutions and, of course, bigger institutions pay their executives more than small banks. But there's also a psychological component: Some bankers are just driven to outmaneuver their competitors and grow faster. It's a compulsion. But these people really aren't bankers. They aren't thinking like bankers. Instead, they're dealmakers. They don't particularly care about managing their institutions; they just want to grow them. And they did just that, growing them to the point that they became, some years ago, "too big to fail." That's a sad statement in a country built on the capitalist notion that companies that can't run their operations correctly go out of business to be replaced by better-managed firms. It seems to me that if you're "too big to fail" you're also, by definition, "too big to succeed." Corporate leaders, confident their institutions are so big that the government will bail them out no matter what risky or foolish moves they make, are going to make risky and foolish moves. Regulations were put in place a long time ago to restrict that kind of unbridled growth, and had regulators enforced the rules instead of tossing them out the window, we wouldn't be in the mess we're in today. Canada and India have strict regulations, and they enforce them. And, as such, they aren't in nearly the sad shape we now find ourselves.

One of the most important laws that wasn't enforced was the Glass-Steagall Act, passed during The Great Depression, which prohibited banks from also dealing in securities like stocks and bonds. Glass-Steagall is the reason that for many years afterwards there was a J.P. Morgan, which was a bank, and a Morgan Stanley, an investment firm. They had both been part of John Pierpont Morgan's financial empire before the Depression. But banks shouldn't be taking the kinds of risks investment firms take, and investment firms can't do the kinds of deals they do if they are confined to the kind of conservative business model that should govern banks. But in their quest to grow, modern day bankers just couldn't stand the idea of not getting in on the lucrative investment business and persuaded Congress and the regulators to let them buy or merge with investment firms. Just as anyone could have predicted — and, in fact, I did predict — letting banks get into the risky investment led straight to the troubles we have today.

I'm writing *Big Bad Banks* because I think the public deserves to know in clear, down-to-earth terms what happened to our savings, to our jobs, and to our country. I'm both sad and embarrassed at the mess my beloved industry has created. Banking has been good to me and my family, and the communities in which we operate. So you can't imagine how painful it has been for me to sit before Congressional committees alongside big-time bankers and be rebuked for the problems the banking industry has created for everyone. I had nothing to do with those problems and had warned often and loudly of where we were headed if things stayed on the course the big banks were setting. I hope *Big Bad Banks* shows you how things went wrong and suggests ways we can eventually get back on track and return to prosperity.

This book, which is really a short history of banking, begins with my entry into the business and ends with President Barack Obama and the Congress trying to repair the damage and ensure that a disaster like this never happens again. The roots of the crisis that has engulfed us took hold slowly at first, although we had ample warning about the dangers of unregulated or poorly regulated financial institutions, first in the Great Depression and then again in the S&L crisis. We ignored those warnings under the guise of letting a free market work its wonders. You won't find a more dedicated capitalist than me, but I know that there must be regulations to encourage competition. If you let too much power (and money) accumulate in too few hands, there will be problems. It's simply human nature for some people to push the limits of whatever they do to the point that the limits break and cause great damage.

How that happened is what this book is about. It encompasses larger-than-life people like Alan Greenspan and Sandy Weill, powerful institutions like Citigroup and the Federal Reserve, and momentous events with unintended consequences.

PART I

Warning signs

Chapter One

In the beginning

I 'm not sure anybody sets out as a child to become a banker. I certainly didn't. Perry Mason, the television lawyer, was my hero and law school was my goal. But in 1964, my first year at Nicholls State University in Thibodaux, La., I took Economics 101. I surprised myself that I enjoyed the course so much and I probably surprised Prof. Rodriguez, too, because I did so well in the course. In any case, part way through the semester he asked me to drop by his office. Would I be interested in taking part in a program sponsored by the Louisiana Bankers Association aimed at encouraging young people to get into banking? That was the classic no-brainer. Banks had air conditioning and the only other jobs I would be likely to land in that summer after my first year of college would be working hard outdoors in Louisiana's blistering heat. I went to work at Citizens National Bank of Morgan City, a one-office bank with just $17 million in assets. The job was simple bookkeeping, but I thoroughly enjoyed the calm, dignified atmosphere of the bank. When I began my second year of college, I switched my major to finance and economics.

I went to school the next summer and didn't work at the bank. But when I applied for a summer job the next year I was taken on as a teller, the first time I had real responsibility for dealing with the public. I loved sitting at the teller's window making small talk with all the customers who came in. One day I looked up and was startled to see standing in front of me Jerry Kramer and Jimmy Taylor, players for the champion Green Bay Packers. They owned a company called Packer Diving and Salvage in Morgan City that did underwater work for the oil and gas industry in the Gulf of Mexico. I had a ball listening to their stories about the Packers, and Kramer gave me a copy of his book. At the end of that summer I knew banking was what I wanted to do.

I guess the bank was as happy with me as I was with it because even before I finished my degree the bank took me on part-time in the collections department. I also was put in charge of the new walk-up window, where we handled transactions for people after the bank's office had closed at 4 p.m. In 1969, after fulfilling my National Guard commitment, I was hired full time and worked in collections and the note department for the next two years. Doing collections was an eye-opening experience for me. I had been brought up to trust people, but I quickly discovered that you can't trust everybody. I learned to discern the people who were having problems repaying loans because of job loss, medical problems, or other unforeseen circumstances, from the deadbeats who took the bank's money with no intention of repaying it. Since then, I've made it a principle to help people rearrange their loan terms when they had a good reason for defaulting and go after the real deadbeats with everything I can, including hauling them into court. Fortunately my instincts and the bank's strict lending standards keep the number of court dates to a minimum.

In 1971, Herb Stire, the president of Citizens National, asked me to help get the bank involved in small business lending and credit cards. I jumped at the chance, and he began very patiently teaching me the loan business. At first, about all I did was attend meetings with him and potential borrowers and run documents around to get the needed signatures. I honestly thought it was a big waste of my time and the bank's money. Only later did I realize that I was being indoctrinated into the core of the banking business. Gradually I began picking up more responsibility, making SBA and other small loans under the constant scrutiny of Stire and his senior officers. After a few years of that I was thrilled when the bank named me assistant cashier. I was a bank officer!

It was about then that I began thinking like a businessman. As part of my National Guard obligation, I had to do weekend training in Franklin, La., about 35 miles from Morgan City. During the bull sessions that were part of those weekends I would listen to some of my buddies complain about the two banks in Franklin. They were both run by aristocratic, old-line families who didn't seem to care much about their customers, the regular folks in town. I would go back to work on Monday after the weekend training and tell Stire and others that we ought to open a branch in Franklin because I knew we treated our customers a lot better than those two banks. Like Morgan City, Franklin was in St. Mary Parish (a parish is Louisiana's equivalent of counties in other states), and at first Stire rejected my idea. Banks in the same parish just didn't muscle in on one another's territory. But I kept coming back to work with anecdotes of Franklin bankers' poor customer service, and eventually Stire began to think about it. But he wasn't just going to take my word for it. He hired a business professor from Louisiana State University to do a competitive market study. The professor came back and told us that we would almost certainly be able to turn a profit in the Franklin market after five years. That sounded like a long time to me, but Stire decided we should move ahead. In 1973, after an acrimonious board battle that saw one director resign rather than "poach" on another bank's territory, we were going to Franklin. More importantly, Stire told me to head up the new office in Franklin. Here I was at 26 years old, a wife and baby at home, and I was being given a job that could make or break our bank.

Within a week I was in Franklin, supervising the purchase of a trailer to serve as our temporary office and hiring a staff. Rather than commute 35 miles each way every day I decided the Cloutier family needed to be a very visible part of the community in Franklin, so we picked up and moved there. For the next couple of years the family didn't see much of me. I was immersed in the community, attending every event — even serving as the announcer for the Friday night high school football games. I was a fixture in Little League, Biddy Basketball, and every other civic endeavor you can imagine. The Louisiana Jaycees named me one of the outstanding young men in the state. It took only one year for our Franklin branch to exceed its 10-year plan on virtually every measure.

Meanwhile, across the region, business activity was heat-ing up. Though I can't say Jimmy Carter was one of America's best presidents, I freely admit that Louisiana was a huge beneficiary of Carter's effort to wean the United States off foreign oil. His policies sparked a huge economic boom in the state as oil and gas exploration took off. It was a heady time for many, but my economics background told me we were experiencing a bubble that just couldn't last. Nobody wanted to hear that, though, and I was soon labeled "Dr. Doom" for my frequent warnings that the good times wouldn't keep rolling.

I got my first inkling of the troubles that lay ahead for banking during that boom time. By 1981, I had returned to Morgan City as a vice president and a senior loan officer. Morgan City is a small town, and I knew who among the businesses at the core of its economy was creditworthy and who wasn't. I always felt bad when I had to turn down a potential borrower, but the bank's safety was paramount. By then, however, the national expansion of banking was getting under way, and I noticed the customers I had turned down for a loan got one anyway — and not from the local banks that competed with us. They had pretty much the same standards as we did. If I wouldn't lend you money, chances are that none of the other banks was going to take that risk, either.

I particularly remember my friend, Bucky (I won't use his real name to avoid embarrassing him). Bucky was a boat broker and a pretty good one. You have to understand that in Morgan City, when we talk about boats and brokers, we aren't talking about yachts in Fort Lauderdale or Houston and the carefully groomed men and women who sell them. Bucky brokered workboats and barges, the massive vessels that delivered supplies and people to the big rigs working out in the Gulf. But like so many people during the oil boom, Bucky got greedy.

"I don't see why the boat owners should be making millions and I'm not," he told me when he applied for a $125,000 loan to build a barge. Like I said, Bucky was a friend and we had done business with him for years so I believed that even though he was a good boat broker, he wasn't the kind of careful businessman our bank wanted to lend money to. He didn't speak to me for a few weeks after I turned him down, but then one day he called me.

"I want to show you how real bankers operate," he told me. He picked me up a short while later and we drove out to the nearby airport. At the appointed hour, a small, twin-engine private plane landed, and two young men in expensive suits with briefcases got out. While I stood in the background watching, Bucky and the two bankers from Continental Illinois National Bank and Trust Company bent over the hood of Bucky's car and signed the papers for a $125,000 loan to build a barge. They hadn't done a credit check and didn't ask for any collateral. Then they got in their plane and flew off. The entire transaction took less than 15 minutes. I knew one of two things at that point: either I was way too conservative to play in the big leagues, or that loan was going to go bust. Turns out, I wasn't too conservative, and two years later Bucky was bust.

But that was just the beginning. A few months after the airport loan, I got a call from another Continental Illinois banker offering to buy my "turn down" list of loan applicants I had rejected. He told me his bank had retained McKinsey & Co. as a consultant to help the bank grow, and McKinsey told them to get into the oil and gas business in Louisiana and Texas. Obviously a lot of people were thinking bigger was better.

Meanwhile, I was perfectly happy being a banker in Morgan City. But I got a phone call one day in July 1984 from a group of business people in Lafayette, La., about 60 miles away, who were starting a bank. Would I serve as president and CEO? Talk about stunned. I was just 37 years old and was being offered the top operational job at a new bank. At first it was a little overwhelming, but I was confident that I could lead people effectively and, while there was always more to learn, I knew a lot about banking. I had always wanted to run my own company so I jumped at the chance and became president and CEO of MidSouth Bank.

When I took that new job in 1984, the boom had fizzled out. The bankers I knew all had a favorite saying: "Stay alive 'til '85." It was their way to look ahead to better times for the ailing oil and gas industry. But the times didn't get better: In 1986, unemployment in Lafayette hit an astounding 26 percent and more than a few of the banks in Louisiana and Texas didn't stay alive beyond '85 and many more failed in the years afterward. We were constantly getting calls from the Federal Deposit Insurance Corporation's Memphis regional office asking us to come up and look over the books of banks that were on the verge of failure and needed to be bought by healthier institutions. I looked at many, but bought only two, both of which were in Lafayette and thus known entities to me: Breaux Bridge Bank and Trust Co. and Commerce and Industry Bank. Even then our survival was sometimes questionable and it turned out that our biggest problem wasn't bad loans in the oil and gas business, but in real estate. When a borrower in the oil and gas industry went under we could always sell the equipment to recoup a good portion of the loan we had made. Sometimes we had to market that equipment in China or South America, but we could always find a buyer. Not so with real estate. You couldn't move real estate to somewhere else. As people fell behind on their notes they would offer a house or a commercial building at a steeply discounted price and that hurt the price of every other piece of real estate in the area. Lots that had sold for $75,000 in 1983 were bringing just $10,000 in the late 1980s and condos that had sold for $125,000 were bringing just $30,000. And that was when they could find a buyer. Many just sat on the market attracting no offers at all. It was that painful, near-death experience that made me extremely wary throughout the rest of my career about the dangers of real estate lending and amplified my concerns about what I was seeing as banks got bigger and bigger and engaged in riskier practices.

But we survived and, when it was all over, we even thrived. The downturn ended for us in 1991 and by 1993 we were able to take MidSouth Bank public, the smallest bank — $86 million in assets and a market cap of just $4 million (talk about small-cap stocks!) — ever to be listed on a major stock exchange (symbol: MSL). The bank continued to grow over the next 15 years and today we have more than $930 million in assets, 35 locations covering most of South Louisiana and Southeast Texas, and an online presence at www.midsouthbank.com.

Chapter Two

THE SAVINGS AND LOAN CRISIS

I f you think banking should be simple, you ought to go back and look at the way the old savings and loan industry operated before it blew up in the 1980s. That was about as simple as it can get. The S&Ls took in deposits, primarily from local people trying to save a buck for a rainy day, and lent it out as mortgages to people who wanted to buy a house. Most of the S&Ls up to the middle 1970s were homegrown institutions that confined business mostly to their communities. Partly, it was because they were strictly regulated and could offer only low rates of return to depositors and only certain types of very conservative mortgages to borrowers. Still, for the local businesspeople who were part of the S&L industry, it was a pretty cushy life. The risks weren't high, and some of the toughest decisions the officers of a local S&L had to make were what brands of toasters they would offer as premiums to attract depositors.

But that cushy life suddenly got a lot tougher in the late 1970s when the Organization of the Petroleum Exporting Countries tightened the oil spigot. Energy prices went through

the roof and helped touch off a period of sustained high inflation. High inflation almost always brings with it high long-
term interest rates. Inflation and interest rates are tied together because lenders know that the value of a dollar lent today
will be a lot less when it's repaid years later. To make up for that
reduced value, the lender naturally wants to crank up the interest rate he charges the borrower. What's more, the people
who are depositing money with the lender naturally want to
protect the value of their deposits, too, so they will put their
money only in an institution that offers a high rate of return.
The problem became more complicated with the advent of
money market funds, a product Wall Street invented that allowed brokerage firms and mutual funds to pay interest rates
higher than banks and S&Ls were allowed to charge. That, of
course, prompted millions of investors to move their money
out of banks and S&Ls and into the money market funds. That
was a big problem for the banking industry. Had Congress
chosen to regulate money market funds the way the banks and
S&Ls were governed, the problem would have been solved.
But instead, Congress and the Carter administration elected
to relax the caps on the banks and S&Ls. Suddenly, banks and
S&Ls were pitted directly against Wall Street.

It was an unfair fight. The obvious result was that depositors getting 2 percent interest on their accounts at the local
S&L saw a mutual fund offering 8 percent and they scurried to
take their money out of the S&L and deposit it in the fund. All
of a sudden the S&Ls and many banks were being starved for
funds to lend. To make matters worse, the low-interest loans
they had made to home buyers and real estate developers in

their communities were a lot less valuable. Mortgage loans are often sold among financial institutions, but what financial executive would pay full price for a loan with a 4 percent return on it when interest rates everywhere else were 8 percent or higher? So the mortgage loans the S&Ls had made could be sold only at steep discounts, and the value of the loans they kept on their books — in essence, their assets — was reduced, too. It was a double whammy that threatened to sink the entire S&L industry.

The efforts by the Carter administration and Congress to help the banks and S&Ls pretty much failed. When Carter left office in 1981, an estimated 3,300 of the 3,800 S&Ls were losing money. But when Congress tried to ride to the rescue, the problems really began. The Garn-St. Germain Depository Institutions Act of 1982 went much further than had Carter in giving S&Ls more flexibility. They could pay higher rates for deposits, borrow from the Federal Reserve, make commercial loans, and even issue credit cards. If that sounds like a bank, you're right. The S&Ls were transforming themselves into commercial banks. They were even allowed to take an ownership stake in the real estate developments to which they previously had only been allowed to lend money.

The stage was set for disaster. One of the things that typically accompanies high inflation is a real estate boom on the theory that property — remember, they aren't making any more of it — won't lose its value the way currency will because the government can print as many dollar bills as it wants. So in the early '80s interest rates were high and real estate prices were rising. The S&L guys jumped in with both feet, lending money willy-nilly to real estate ventures near and far and buying big stakes in some of the developments. Trouble was, a lot of S&L executives didn't know much about real estate development and they certainly knew even less about real estate in other markets. In addition to the clueless S&L executives, the industry, with its rapidly increasing profits, attracted more than its fair share of scammers. Of course, banks weren't innocent bystanders during this period. The big banks were lending money to real estate developers even faster than the S&Ls. Some amazingly bad ideas got financing: condos overlooking trash dumps, office buildings miles from the nearest town, and multiple shopping centers in towns too small to support one mall.

Even as the S&L industry and the banks were wallowing in inflationary money, Federal Reserve Chairman Paul Volcker was vowing to break the back of inflation. I knew he was serious and it was one of the reasons I kept predicting that the good times were going to end. To quell inflation, Volcker essentially decided to push the economy into a recession by raising short-term interest rates until businesses simply couldn't afford to borrow any more to expand. And if businesses don't expand, they usually contract. That means layoffs, plant closings, empty shopping malls, and all the other ill effects that characterize a recession. As I surveyed the scene in 1980 I knew that if I were a betting man, I'd back Volcker. And if my bet won, that meant the S&L folks would lose their shirts. My guy won.

Sure enough, the economy went into a fairly serious recession. People fearful for their jobs quit buying houses, cars, appliances, and most everything else. Companies didn't need bigger headquarters, there weren't any shoppers to come to the malls and suddenly the banks and S&Ls had a huge pile of bad loans on their books. Both banks and S&Ls began to sink under the weight of those bad loans.

The S&L crisis, curiously enough, reinforced my confidence in my own judgment. Here's how: I was sitting in my office at the bank one Wednesday when my secretary came in to tell me that one of the regulators who often visited the bank wanted to see me. I wondered what was up, as they usually start their audits on Mondays. When he came into my office he said this wasn't about an audit. He had been informed that over the past few years we would occasionally warn the regulators about the risky loans big banks like Continental Illinois were making in our territory, loans like the one Bucky got for his barges. Those complaints had seemed to fall on deaf ears. Don't worry about it, we were told, you don't understand the complexity of major banking in America. But now they were getting interested in what we had to say. The examiner visiting me knew there were problems in the system and wanted to know more. Finally he looked at me and asked "Do you know what we call a bank that has 5 percent bad loans and 6 percent capital?"

I shook my head.

"Insolvent," he said.

As he was leaving he asked me if I had ever heard of a bank called Penn Square. I told him no, I didn't know that name.

"You will soon," he said with an enigmatic smile.

Shortly afterward, Penn Square Bank collapsed in 1982

and sparked the banking crisis of the 1980s by dragging down Continental Illinois with the weight of its bad loans. Federal regulators were prepared to see it fail in order to send a message to other banks about risky lending, but some congressmen and editorial boards weighed in that Continental Illinois was "too big to fail," and regulators essentially were forced to offer the bank a $4.5 billion rescue package in 1984.

I had been in my career for 15 years and the banking crisis that I had seen coming confirmed that I knew my business. It also confirmed, though, that optimism can be misplaced. I assumed that the problems that led to the crisis would soon be fixed and things would return to normal: banking would be conservative and safe. That didn't happen.

Between 1980 and 1983 a total of 118 S&Ls failed, and the number would have been much higher if the Reagan administration, fearful of the message it would send to shutter hundreds of S&Ls, had not encouraged and even forced sick S&Ls to merge with one another to try to bolster their financial standings. That only delayed the worst of the S&L crisis, and it took several years for the full extent of the incompetence and corruption to become evident. I know a guy who took over one S&L that had been started in 1979. It was closed in 1984. After it was all over, I mentioned to him that it seemed to happen very fast. Oh, he told me, it happened a lot faster than you think. "We opened at 9 o'clock the first day and bought a lot of loans all over the country and were broke by lunch on the first day. It just took us four years to realize it."

When it became clear that there were still hundreds of S&Ls that couldn't survive without government life support,

Congress decided the nation couldn't afford to just let them collapse. Understand, not one of the ailing S&Ls was, by itself, "too big to fail." But it was the political judgment of Congress that as an industry they were too big to fail. So the taxpayers bailed them out to the tune of $124 billion. My bank and thousands of other community banks are still paying that bill through increased deposit insurance rates.

Along the way some prominent political names emerged from the wreckage. Sen. John McCain, for example, was a member of the notorious Keating Five, a group of five senators accused of interfering with a federal investigation of a failed California S&L, a scheme that drew rebuke from the Senate Ethics Committee. And there was Neil Bush, son of Vice President George H.W. Bush, who, as a director of the failing Silverado Savings and Loan, approved $100 million in loans to two business partners. The loans failed, the U.S. Office of Thrift Supervision accused Neil Bush of "multiple conflicts of interest," and he paid a $50,000 fine and was banned from banking for his role in Silverado's collapse, which cost taxpayers $1.3 billion.

As I sit here today pondering the situation we find ourselves in, I keep thinking back to the bad days of the early 1980s when it seemed things were just falling apart. The financial industry was on its knees. Suddenly, the government was getting into the business of rescuing private enterprise, bailing out Continental Illinois Bank as well as Chrysler Corp., the nation's third largest automaker. It was a shocking time for me, compounded by the downturn in the oil industry that pounded the Louisiana economy. And now, of course, we're facing the same situation — only much worse.

I assumed at the time that we had all learned some valuable lessons from the traumatic experiences of the early 1980s. One is that we should use regulations wisely. Regulations are put in place for a reason, usually to force businesses to be prudent and responsible. If you change them to benefit the businesses that are regulated, you can pretty well be sure that those businesses are going to exploit the looser regulatory environment in every way they can. Just count on greed and ego trumping good business sense and leading to big problems. Sure, had we kept the strict regulations on the S&L industry it might have died. But it ended up dying anyway. The regulations would have killed it much sooner, and its death would have been much less traumatic for the nation.

I also thought we had learned that we can't allow any institution to get too big to fail. But of course "too big to fail" is both an economic and a political concept. In the early 1980s neither Continental Illinois nor Chrysler were "too big to fail" in the economic sense. Both were bailed out solely on the basis of politics. Their failure would not have materially harmed the economy. In fact, one can argue that had Chrysler been allowed to go under, both General Motors and Ford would have been healthier since they would have picked up the vast majority of Chrysler's market share. Is it possible that by rescuing Chrysler in the early 1980s we doomed GM to bankruptcy in 2009? I always marvel at the law of unintended consequences. We cannot know all the effects that our actions will have in the future.

PART II

Instruments and Agents of Destruction

Chapter Three

THE AMERICAN NIGHTMARE

In the end, of course, people were the root cause of the financial crisis that almost wrecked the global economy. I'll explain the problems created by people like Alan Greenspan, Sandy Weill, and Phil Gramm shortly. But when I think about how the crisis happened I keep being reminded of the saying gun lobbyists use to fight restrictions on guns: "Guns don't kill people; people do." I agree completely, but we can't lose sight of the fact that if the people didn't have the guns they might not have killed anyone. And if the people who created the financial crisis didn't have the weapons to do it, it might not have happened. What's particularly ironic is that the weapons in this case started out as important and useful tools in the nation's economy, but grew into deadly monsters that swept through the economy, wreaking havoc on ordinary Americans as well as the world's most powerful financial institutions.

The two weapons I refer to are credit cards and home mortgages. What is particularly interesting in the case of these two very common products is that the big banks and other financial institutions not only used credit cards and mortgage loans to hurt ordinary people while profiting hugely, but then they wound up turning the weapons on themselves, too. More about how that happened in the next chapter. But first let me explain the evolution of credit cards and mortgages from their very conservative origins up to the point that the financial institutions began shooting themselves with these products.

Credit cards were first offered widely some 40 years ago as a convenience to banks' retail customers. With a credit card you needn't carry big wads of cash. As an incentive to repay that credit card debt promptly, the banks usually assessed the highest interest rates they could under the various state laws governing usury. Banks were also pretty careful about issuing credit cards. Generally speaking, you needed to prove your income and have some modicum of assets before your local bank would give you a credit card. Indeed, for a long time having a credit card was an indication that you had arrived at a certain level of financial success.

But that all began to change in 1978 when the Supreme Court, in its Marquette Decision, ruled that usury laws only in the state where a bank is located, not those in the state in which a consumer lives, could be used to set interest-rate ceilings. So, if you were a bank in Florida with a 16 percent cap on interest rates, you could make a loan to a New Yorker, where the cap was 12 percent, and charge her the 16 percent rate allowed by Florida.

The real impact of the Marquette Decision became apparent a year later in South Dakota. In 1979 the Federal Reserve was using extremely high interest rates to combat inflation.

Banks that borrowed from the Fed were paying 20 percent for short-term loans. Like most states, South Dakota had limits on the interest rates banks could charge their customers. But in an effort to encourage local banks to lend more freely, state officials removed those limits, freeing any bank in South Dakota to charge as much as it wanted in interest rates on credit cards, as well as other kinds of loans. That South Dakota decision got a lot of attention back in New York City where Citibank (later to become Citicorp, then Citigroup) was laboring under a 12 percent limit on the interest rate it could charge on credit cards. Walter Wriston, then the chairman of Citibank, promptly set up the bank's credit card operations in South Dakota and began jacking up interest rates. Big competitors quickly followed, and the race was on to milk all the profits they could from credit cards.

CardWeb.com, a credit industry analysis group, estimates the average American today has eight charge cards or accounts and is carrying something like $8,000 in debt, much of that at exorbitant rates. Filing for personal bankruptcy used to be a way to escape the onerous burdens of those debts, but in 2005 the big banks lobbied Congress successfully to make it much more difficult to file for personal bankruptcy. Their argument was that unscrupulous borrowers were charging up huge debts, then just walking away because they could clear those debts through bankruptcy proceedings.

The truth was a little different. Sure, there are some bad egg borrowers out there, millionaires with plenty of income and assets who would hide behind bankruptcy protection. But most cases of personal bankruptcy involve unforeseen expenses, often for medical bills for illnesses or accidents. And you can't tell me that the credit card companies, with all the information they can get on anyone, didn't know in advance if a customer was creditworthy. They sent out millions of credit card applications to people they knew were risky. They encouraged those people to transfer the huge balances on their existing credit cards at teaser rates that didn't last long before the big interest rates kicked in. They were, in essence, encouraging consumers to engage in their own miniature Ponzi schemes by using a new card to pay off the balance on an old card. This kiting of credit resulted in bigger and bigger debts for consumers who thought, or more accurately hoped, the party would never end. But don't kid yourself. The banks that were large issuers of credit cards loved all that accumulated consumer debt because it kept the profits flowing. In the real world those banks would be known as "loan sharks." Two of the biggest credit card issuers, MBNA and Capital One, weren't really even banks. But when Congress began looking into predatory lending practices of credit card issuers a few years ago, a strange thing happened: Bank of America, one of the banks that had become "too big to fail," bought MBNA in 2005 and, even more remarkably, Capital One began buying banks, starting with one of my competitors, Hibernia Bank of New Orleans, also in 2005. Suddenly these institutions that consumer groups have labeled "predatory lenders" and their risky loans were part of our national banking system. Clearly, standards were falling.

Out-of-control credit cards are bad enough, but the real culprit in the current financial crisis has been mortgage lending. For a long time a home mortgage was a classic banking transaction: We took deposits from some customers and lent them to others who hoped to fulfill the American dream of owning a house. We knew the borrowers, their employers, and the neighborhoods where they wanted to buy. If we made the loan, we typically held onto it, collecting the principal and interest to make a small profit. If homeowners got into financial trouble, we often could work out an arrangement that kept them and their families in the house. Those were the good old days.

The mortgage business began to change in the early 1990s under the Clinton administration. Bill Clinton appointed Henry Cisneros to become head of the Department of Housing and Urban Development in 1993, the first Hispanic to run the office. Cisneros knew that low-income families, many of whom were minorities, had a hard time getting a mortgage given the strict lending standards of those days. To try to remedy the problem, he created the National Homeownership Strategy, which allowed the Department of Housing and Urban Development to help first-time home buyers in several ways: it reduced the amount of stable income the borrowers had to show to three years from five; it allowed lenders to hire their own property appraisers instead of using government-approved appraisers; and it scrapped requirements that lenders had to do face to face interviews with a borrower in an office. Although it had long been important for banks to choose only "prime" customers who could repay their mortgages, the new looser requirements tempted many bankers to go after the so-called "subprime" market of borrowers with questionable financial backgrounds.

After George H. W. Bush took office in 1989 and his free market deregulators got to work, the pace of subprime lending picked up sharply. One thing that helped fuel the growing mountain of mortgage debt was the increasing use by banks and other financial institutions of "securitization." In the good old days, when a bank made a mortgage loan it generally held on to the loan and collected the interest payments and principal. But each loan it made required that it go out and get the deposits from other customers to cover that loan. If, instead, the bank could sell that mortgage to someone else, it would get the mortgage off its own books and could then issue another mortgage. The investors who bought the mortgages would pay the bank a fee for doing the administrative work. In essence, the banks decided they wanted the steady stream of fee income from making mortgages more than they wanted the income from the mortgages themselves. For a long time the banks would sell mortgages intact. But then came the idea of securitization, a process that bundles thousands of mortgages and sells that bundle as a kind of bond that pays interest based on the combined interest rates of all those mortgages. This is where it starts to get complicated, so we'll focus on these toxic packages of mortgage debts in the next chapter. Suffice it to say, securitization was like pouring gasoline on a fire: the mortgage business soared. Because the banks and the mortgage companies weren't going to hold the mortgage themselves, they really didn't care whether the borrower could afford to buy the house or not; the banks just wanted to make more loans.

Naturally, credit standards steadily diminished in the Bush years as banks scrambled to make more and more sub-prime loans to unqualified buyers. The result was exactly what anyone in his right mind would expect: unwary or unscrupulous buyers loaded up on mortgage loans they couldn't afford, hoping that an ever-rising real estate market would eventually bail them out.

I think the final race to jump off the cliff in 2008 began on June 17, 2002, with a speech President George W. Bush made at St. Paul AME Church, an historic African-American church in Atlanta. As chairman of the advisory board of Federal National Mortgage Association (known colloquially as Fannie Mae), I was sitting in the third pew from the front as the president described what he believed was a big problem in America: "Too many American families, too many minorities, do not own a home. There is a home ownership gap in America. The difference between Anglo-American and Hispanic home ownership is too big. And we've got to focus the attention of this nation to address this. And it starts with setting a goal. And so by the year 2010, we must increase minority homeowners by at least 5.5 million. In order to close the homeownership gap, we've got to set a big goal for America, and focus our attention and resources on that goal." He said he wanted to see more money flow into low-income housing and he wanted the mortgage industry to find a way to make it easier to buy a home.

The mortgage business had been growing before that, but now the president's message to bankers was simple: lend, lend, lend! The big banks and brokerage firms fought furiously with one another to find faster and easier ways to get people into houses. Their eagerness, in turn, prompted hundreds of thousands of small-time entrepreneurs to become mortgage brokers. Anyone who wanted to could put up a sign that said "mortgage loan office." It was easier to open a mortgage office than it was to become a bail bondsman. As fast as the brokers would generate a loan, the Wall Street banks would fight to buy it and securitize it while the broker just turned around and signed up another borrower. Despite the immense increase in mortgage credit, the Federal Reserve didn't do any checking on the qualifications of the people selling the loans, and the Securities and Exchange Commission asked no questions about the quality of the loans being packaged and sold by the big banks' brokerage firms. Never in history has there been so little oversight given to such a large expansion of credit. When state attorneys general, led by New York's Eliot Spitzer, tried to take action against "predatory lenders," George W. Bush's administration not only didn't help, it even used the Office of the Comptroller of the Currency to invoke an old law that forbade the states from going after the bad guys.

In its frantic scramble to grab market share, the Wall Street crowd kept coming up with one "innovation" after another to make the process faster and easier. First was the "no down payment loan" that gave the homebuyer 100 percent of the loan. Then came extended loans: If the bank didn't think borrowers could pay back loans in 25 or 30 years, it gave them 40-year loans. The next bright new idea was the "interest-only loan," for homebuyers who couldn't afford to pay down the balance of the loan. "Balloon loans" gave borrowers artificially low loan payments for the first few years of their mortgage and then stuck them with a big increase in payments to make up for the increased principal they would then owe. "No doc" loans that didn't require any documentation of a borrower's income or assets were followed quickly by so-called "liar loans" that let borrowers simply make up information about their financial situation.

Although the president's message in 2002 was aimed at getting more minorities into their own homes, a goal it certainly accomplished, it wasn't just poor people who took advantage of the easy terms. The demand for housing fueled a big increase in prices. Speculators, anyone from lawyers to housewives, grabbed at the easy money to buy and flip houses and condos in such desirable areas as California, Arizona, and Florida. A 200-unit condo on Biscayne Bay in Miami would be sold out before the foundation was even in place. By the time the building was complete, most of the condos had already been sold two or three times at ever-higher prices. It seemed incredible: The banking industry had found a new way to create vast amounts of wealth, with everyone getting rich on the rising value of real estate.

To get as much of the new pot of gold as they possibly could, everyone in the mortgage business wanted to speed up the process. One way to do that was "table top approvals." A bank would set up its own computer in the mortgage broker's office to grant loan approvals on the spot and nearly instantly. Some old-school bankers still wanted to ask borrowers questions about their jobs, incomes, debts, etc. But all that talk, talk, talk was slowing down the system. Instead of asking for income verification, just ask the guy how much money he makes. So what if he lies; it won't be any skin off our back. Everyone was now being driven by his or her bonus payouts. The more loans they could make, the more profit they could generate and the bigger the bonuses that they would receive.

And, of course, it all ended. Rising defaults on subprime mortgages were the beginning of the end. And, as these things do, it ended rather quickly. People started thinking twice about buying that new house or condo, refinancing their existing one, or trying to flip properties. As demand quickly ebbed, so did prices. Falling prices, in turn, scared more people, and the whole thing became a self-fulfilling prophecy on the downside just as the bubble had been the result of a self-fulfilling prophecy — house prices will always rise! — on the upside. Millions of people found themselves making mortgage payments on a house that wasn't worth what they owed on it. Not surprisingly, many simply walked away. That, in turn, triggered the massive collapse of big financial institutions, as I will explain momentarily.

I know it sounds old-fashioned, but there were two things missing in the mortgage imbroglio: reality and accountability. As house prices soared everyone became convinced that the boom would go on forever and no one was accountable for anything. The mortgage broker collected his fee, while the Wall Street banker packaged the loans and sold them to investors who should have known better. Homeowners or speculators who took advantage of the easy financing weren't really buying a house. Instead, they were buying an option on a house. If they lost their job or otherwise couldn't keep up payments, they simply walked away. Of course, reality and accountability would have destroyed the giant money machine, which is exactly what happened when the bubble finally burst. The American Dream became the American Nightmare.

Chapter Four

A FRONT-ROW SEAT

I liked Frank Raines as soon as I met him in the late 1990s. He had just left the Clinton administration, where he had served as chief budget officer and he was justifiably proud that the administration had balanced the budget and the talk on Wall Street was all about how soon the government was going to pay off the entire deficit. Raines also represented a class of highly educated African-Americans who had risen to high positions of responsibility. When I met him he was heading for the next step up the rung, chief executive of the Federal National Mortgage Association, known as Fannie Mae. I thought Raines well deserved the job and that Fannie Mae would continue to fulfill its mission of helping middle-class Americans afford homes.

Fannie Mae and its much younger competitor, the Federal Home Loan Mortgage Corporation, known as Freddie Mac, were odd animals. The government established Fannie Mae in 1938 to issue and insure bonds on home loans so that people could obtain mortgages. For most of its history Fannie Mae acted as a middleman, buying mortgage loans made by banks and savings and loan institutions and in turn reselling them to big investors, such as insurance companies that wanted safe, long-term returns.

It was a pretty simple business plan: Say a young couple wanted to buy a $35,000 home. A bank would demand 20 percent down and would carefully review the couple's job history, income, and debt levels. If the borrowers passed the review, the bank would lend them the $28,000 that represented 80 percent of the purchase price. Fannie Mae would pay the bank a fee for having put the loan together, then it would turn around and sell the loan to an insurance company. If the initial interest rate on the loan was 6 percent, Fannie would sell it to the insurance company with an interest rate of 5.5 percent, keeping half a percent for itself. The insurance company was delighted because it had collected premiums from people buying life insurance, perhaps even the same couple who bought the house. Using the premiums to buy the loan made great financial sense for the insurance company. It had a very safe return of 5.5 percent on a 30-year mortgage, and it was likely that it wouldn't have to pay a life insurance claim on the young couple for 40 or more years. Fannie Mae made money on the sale of the loan, the insurance company received a good long-term stream of payments and the couple had the house of their dreams. That was the classic mortgage scenario I talked about in the last chapter, and Fannie Mae was an important part of it. From its inception up until 2008, Fannie Mae put an estimated 55 million families in homes.

But in 1968 a fundamental change occurred in Fannie Mae's structure. The federal government, eager to shore up the budget, converted Fannie Mae into a private shareholder-owned corporation. It became what is called a government-sponsored enterprise, or GSE. Two years later the government created Freddie Mac to compete with Fannie Mae and it, too, became a GSE. Now here's the thing that distinguished Fannie Mae and Freddie Mac from other players in the financial business: Because of their status as GSEs, everyone assumed that the federal government would put its full faith and credit behind the two companies. And because people assumed that would be the case, Fannie and Freddie were able to borrow money at very low rates because they effectively were backed by the government and couldn't fail. But if you examined the situation carefully, you couldn't find anywhere a written statement that the government would back either company if it were in danger of failing. Of course, not many people looked very carefully, and everybody just went along doing business as if Fannie and Freddie had some sort of absolute guarantee against failure. When Raines took over at Fannie Mae, the winds of change had already swept over the financial industry with the passage of new laws that opened up the markets in amazing ways. The big banks were being deregulated and were competing in more markets and with more products than anyone would have thought possible — including totally unregulated derivatives.

Raines's predecessor at Fannie Mae, James Johnson, had done a spectacular job of growing Fannie Mae into one of the nation's largest companies. He did that in part through aggressive business practices, but also by building a powerful political machine that could protect Fannie Mae's interests.

The big banks didn't like the GSEs being in the same business as they were with the built-in advantage of that presumed government backing. And those in Congress who were backed by the big banks obviously were interested in protecting their big contributors against the GSEs.

I wasn't the least bit naïve when Raines asked me in 2001 to sit on the Fannie Mae National Advisory Council, made up of about 35 of the leading homebuilders, bankers, mortgage companies, public housing groups, and consumer groups. I was asked to join for two reasons. First, I was rising in the leadership at the Independent Community Bankers of America, where I was scheduled to become chairman in two years. ICBA had always been a big supporter of Fannie and Freddie because so many small banks depended on the GSEs to buy the mortgages the banks originated. I was also asked because I was from Louisiana and was close to our legislators, including Rep. Richard Baker, who had sort of a love-hate relationship with the GSEs; Rep. Billy Tauzin, head of the House Commerce Committee; and Rep. Jim McCrery, a rising star on the Ways and Means Committee. My role was to go before Congress to defend Fannie Mae from the accusations of a group called FM Watch that was continually trying to raise concerns that if Fannie Mae got into trouble, the failure could cause huge losses to the U.S. Treasury. Now don't get me wrong, I thought all along that it was important for Fannie Mae to adhere to strict financial guidelines like any good conservative bank. If it did, there wouldn't be any trouble. What really irked me was that the members of FM Watch weren't concerned citizens; they were the big banks and giant Wall Street firms that wanted to eliminate Fannie Mae so they wouldn't have competition. They made their usual pitch that the market would take care of itself and government shouldn't be interfering through the GSEs.

Then Raines invited me to attend the speech that President Bush gave in Atlanta. You'll recall from the last chapter that Bush set a target of increasing minority home ownership by 5.5 million by 2010. He specifically stated that Fannie Mae would establish partnerships with 100 faith-based organizations to work toward getting more minorities into their own homes. Given that the big banks had been unleashed and allowed to do things that ultimately endangered not only their own existence, but the health of the global financial system, I had thought all along that Raines would be wise to keep Fannie Mae on the path of righteousness, helping people afford homeownership. After all, it was a pretty lucrative franchise Fannie Mae had. But when President Bush invited Raines to fly back to Washington on Air Force One after the speech, I had never seen Raines more elated. He was grinning like the Cheshire Cat. I mistook that grin for happiness, but I've since come to believe it was the grin of greed. For my part, I couldn't help but wonder if Bush's speech was akin to one President Carter had made many years earlier when he promised the country we would be free of foreign oil within 10 years. The oil industry believed that promise and pushed hard to achieve the goal, only to find itself broke eight years later.

It was like Bush's speech had freed Raines from any constraints. From that moment on his focus was to make more money, both for Fannie Mae and for Frank Raines. When the

Fannie Mae National Advisory Council met in Washington in late 2002, the biggest question in Raines's mind seemed to be how to get bankers to stop asking all those pesky questions of people who wanted to borrow money. You have to remember that the community banks like mine were still doing business the old-fashioned way. That meant we worried about whether a borrower would repay the loan and whether the property was sound. The big boys weren't thinking that way. They were just pushing money out the door as fast as they could, as I recounted in the previous chapter. Raines wanted to play in the big leagues and we, the conservative little banks that were Fannie Mae's bread and butter, were making it difficult for him to do that. Raines said all the questions were slowing up the process.

"Why can't bankers understand the word 'approval?'" he asked. He said Fannie Mae would get a loan request and approve it within an hour or two, but the banker at the other end would nevertheless insist on getting tax returns and other documentation from the borrower, even though Fannie Mae had already approved the loan.

The big banks, through FM Watch, continued their "free market" attacks on Fannie Mae and Raines, aided and abetted by the editorial page of *The Wall Street Journal*, which attacked the GSEs ceaselessly as being unfair competitors because of their implicit government backing. (Raines, of course, hated the criticism, especially from *The Wall Street Journal*, but he kept up a good face. One day he flashed a copy of a negative *Journal* story that had his portrait done in the newspaper's distinctive stipple style. The drawing was taken from an old photograph when Raines had more hair. "At least the picture makes me look good," he joked.) But all of that was enough to keep Fannie Mae's stock price lagging behind that of the big banks that were cashing in on the crazy real estate market. That became a real pain in the butt for Raines, at least in part because a higher stock price would justify higher compensation for him. Then he really got upset when the Chicago office of the Federal Home Loan Bank System, which was created to furnish funds for the S&L industry to make mortgage loans, started a program to buy loans and package them for the secondary market, much as Fannie Mae did.

I didn't pull any punches with Raines when he told me he was going to push Congress to forbid the Federal Home Loan Bank System from muscling its way into Fannie Mae's business. Raines would be doing to the FHLBS the exact same thing the big banks were doing to him: trying to eliminate a competitor. The legislators already on the side of the big banks would seize on Raines's hypocrisy and beat him up badly. Besides, I told him, what the Chicago office of the FHLBS was planning to do was pretty small potatoes compared to the massive mortgage business that Fannie Mae had developed. "Just don't worry about it," I told him. "Keep your mind on business." As it turned out, the Chicago office of the FHLBS wound up incurring huge losses, which just goes to prove that almost everybody who chased that business wound up broke.

As a member of the Fannie Mae National Advisory Council, I wasn't always privy to what was going on behind the scenes at Fannie Mae. *The Wall Street Journal* had reported that the SEC was investigating alleged accounting irregularities at

Fannie Mae, but Raines just dismissed those reports as scurrilous rumors. So you can imagine my shock when on Dec. 21, 2004, Raines accepted what he called "early retirement." The Office of Federal Housing Enterprise Oversight, the regulatory body that oversaw the GSEs, accused him of shifting losses in Fannie Mae in such a way that he and his senior executives could collect millions of dollars of undeserved bonuses. The overstated earnings were calculated at $6.3 billion. OFHEO also sued Raines to try to recover some of the $90 million in payments made to him based on the false earnings. Raines, along with two other ranking former executives at Fannie Mae, agreed to pay fines totaling $3 million, which apparently didn't cost Raines a penny since Fannie Mae's insurance policy actually paid them. Raines also agreed to donate $1.8 million from the sale of his Fannie Mae stock to services that help homeowners who are facing foreclosure or other programs to boost homeownership. He also agreed to forgo $5.3 million of "other benefits" related to his pension. In June 2008, *The Wall Street Journal* reported that both Johnson and Raines had received below-market-rate loans from Countrywide Financial, one of the most shameless promoters of dicey subprime mortgages. Fannie Mae was the biggest buyer of Countrywide's mortgages.

I have to agree with the editorial in *The Wall Street Journal* that called Raines's agreement to settle the charges against him a "paltry settlement" that allowed him and the other two executives to "keep the bulk of their riches." The only consolation I have is that Fannie Mae really did do a good job of helping responsible and deserving low-income Americans, including many minorities, realize the dream of homeownership. That's a lot more than I can say about the big banks.

Recall that earlier in this chapter I said that people just assumed that Fannie Mae had the backing of the U.S. government when, in fact, there was no written document guaranteeing its support. Well, in September 2008 all those people who had assumed the government would bail out Fannie Mae if it got into trouble were proved correct. Congress had never explicitly extended government protection to the two GSEs, but that didn't matter. They were teetering on the edge of collapse when the Federal Housing Financial Agency, the regulator that had replaced OFHEO, put Fannie Mae and Freddie Mac into conservatorship, thus making them effectively wards of the state. Of course, there was no gloating from the big banks that had tried so hard to argue that Fannie Mae would put the U.S. Treasury at risk: They were already being bailed out by the government they had purported to despise.

Chapter Five

The Leverage Bomb

A s I noted in the last chapter, one of the most amazing things to me about the financial crisis is how the big banks not only used mortgages and credit cards to hurt ordinary people, but then used those same instruments to blow themselves up. We've seen how the banks and other mortgage lenders, driven by sheer greed, doled out mortgages to any Tom, Dick, or Harry who wanted one with no regard to his ability to make the mortgage payments. That was bad enough and almost certainly would have caused a recession when all those newly minted homeowners began defaulting on their mortgages. But it was what the banks did after they issued those mortgages that really dealt the global financial system a crippling blow. It's all because of a process called "securitization," a process I described briefly earlier in this book.

Let me explain in a little more detail how securitization is supposed to work. Let's say Bank of the Bayou issues 100 mortgages for $100,000 each. It is now owed a total of $1 million by those 100 homeowners. But Bank of the Bayou doesn't want to hold on to those mortgages. It would rather sell them and lend some more money to other homeowners because the fees it collects in writing each mortgage are a good source of profits. So Bank of the Bayou creates a financial instrument — a security, usually a bond — that holds all 100 mortgages and offers it for sale. The investor who buys that security is now entitled to receive the interest and principal payments on those 100 mortgages. The investor didn't have to go out and compete in the market against other lenders to write mortgages. Instead, he simply sits back and collects the income from the mortgages. Of course, he might also suffer any losses if any of the 100 homebuyers default. Simple enough, right? Certainly it was at first, and many banks used the securitization process carefully and profitably.

But then the brilliant boys on Wall Street began to add a new wrinkle. Because their clients had varying appetites for risk and varying needs for different levels of income, the banks, both investment and commercial, began slicing, dicing, and repackaging the portfolios of mortgage loans they bought from lenders. Some of the bank's customers might be much more interested in safety, or the certainty they would be repaid, while others would prefer a little more risk and the higher return that comes with it. The first set of customers would be sold a bond that guaranteed they would be repaid first in the case of defaults. That set of customers would also, however, get a lower interest rate because of that guarantee. At the other extreme, an investor looking for fatter interest payments would have to accept some risk that in case of default he would not be repaid. Each of these chunks of the loan portfolio is called a tranche, the French word for "slice."

Now there is nothing inherently wrong with divvying up a portfolio of loans in that manner. Indeed, it can have a big benefit. When it first issued those 100 mortgages, Bank of the Bayou bore all the risk. By bundling them into a bond and selling that to a Wall Street firm, Bank of the Bayou got rid of that risk and collected a fee. And when the firm bundled those 100 loans with thousands of others it bought from banks nationwide, cut that entire mass of loans up into tranches, then sold them to other clients, the damage that might be done if one of Bank of the Bayou's original borrowers defaulted on his mortgage was spread so widely as to be negligible. Spreading the risk across multiple investors was the justification that the banks used for securitizing all those loans and it was a good justification.

But then they went a step farther down the road to risk. Instead of packaging real loans and selling them as securities the big banks and their cadres of MBAs used all sorts of complex formulas and computing power to create "synthetic" financial instruments that they dubbed collateralized debt obligations. Because these synthetic CDOs were a mishmash of various kinds of loans from different places, the investor who bought them didn't really have a clue what the risk level was. Most didn't care. After all, they just wanted a fat yield. And even those who did care were lulled by yet another engineered product called credit default swaps that the banks and brokers said would act as insurance against any defaults on the CDOs. In their frenzy to make money many billions of dollars worth of face amount of these products were created and sold. Remember, though, that no matter how fancy the name or how much computer and brain power it took to dream up these instruments, underlying them all was the poor homeowner scrambling to make his mortgage payment each month.

And still the big banks and their clients weren't finished. They then added a huge dollop of leverage to this pile of weird financial instruments backed by mortgages, increasing the risk many more times. This is yet another instance in which greed turned a sound idea into something deadly.

Leverage can be and often is used well and properly. When you put down $20,000 to buy a $100,000 house, you're using leverage, or borrowing power. That way you don't have to save the entire $100,000 before you can purchase the house. But leverage can be dangerous if you're not careful. Let's use the $100,000 house as an example. If five years from now you can sell that house for $120,000, you've made $20,000. And how much did you have to invest to earn that $20,000? Only your $20,000 down payment, plus, of course, the monthly payments. That's a very good return on your original investment. But what happens if five years later you can sell the house for only $60,000? Whoops. You have $20,000 equity in the form of your down payment but you still owe nearly $80,000 to the bank. Now you have to come up with $20,000 of your own money to add to the $60,000 sale price to pay off your mortgage.

In terms of the financial crisis, leverage played a dual role. Homeowners with no-money-down mortgages were highly leveraged. They had no equity in the houses they owned. More importantly, the banks and brokers and their clients were putting up very little of the total price of the CDOs and CDSs that they were buying. They were counting on leverage to magnify their returns. In some cases they had only 5 percent of the amount of the loans in cash or other assets. As long as the interest payments underlying the instruments continued unabated they all made huge profits (and the whiz kids and executives were paid enormous bonuses).

Then the party ended.

As all the subprime mortgages made with adjustable rates began to adjust upward, the teaser mortgage payments that had lured the borrowers in the first place rose, too. Suddenly the mortgage payment became very painful. With no equity in their homes, millions of borrowers simply decided to walk away. The nice ones at least mailed the keys to the bank. More than a few trashed the houses before leaving, stealing all the appliances, plumbing fixtures and even the copper wiring. That was the beginning of the end. Big investors around the globe suddenly noticed that default rates on subprime mortgages were soaring. Worse yet, as all those borrowers walked away from their homes there was a sudden glut of unsold homes. It's classic supply-and-demand economics: Too much supply of anything compared to demand and the result is falling prices. And the news that the subprime mortgage market was in trouble suddenly prompted lots more people to think twice about their real estate holdings. Millions decided they didn't need a bigger house or a second house after all. Less demand! Lower prices! For the first time in decades house prices were falling, not rising, in many markets in the United States. In places like Miami, where everybody was buying un-built condos planning to flip them at higher prices, the fast-moving real estate market hit a brick wall. Nobody wanted to buy anything, even at fire-sale prices. More defaults! Lower prices! Panic!

And that same panic slammed head on into the trading floors and executive suites of the big banks and brokers around the world. With mortgage defaults mounting at a dizzying pace, everyone started trying to figure out how to get rid of those CDOs and CDSs. Lots of supply, no demand! Once again, falling prices. But because nobody really understood what exactly was in those CDOs and CDSs — remember, they were synthetic, and only the people who created them had a clue what was behind them (and even many of them didn't know) — the problem was nobody knew what their price should be. Not surprisingly, under those circumstances no one was going to buy them.

In March 2008, the brokerage firm of Bear Stearns was the first to go. Rather than let the firm fail outright the Federal Reserve engineered a deal in which JPMorgan acquired Bear for pennies on the dollar. But Bear's virtual collapse created huge concerns among everyone else in high finance. Was it safe to trade with Lehman Brothers? With Merrill Lynch? As amazing as it seemed, even those giants of finance might be in danger of collapse. And, as it turned out, they were. Lehman Brothers failed in September 2008. The Fed declined to bail out or arrange a purchase of Lehman as a lesson to other banks about the dangers of leverage. As appealing as it might have been to teach them a lesson, it was a bad idea. Lehman's collapse terrified everyone and financial markets ceased to function, exacerbating an already deep recession and forcing the U.S. government to scramble to devise ways of saving the global financial system. Even the insurance giant AIG was brought to its knees as a result of the credit default insurance derivatives on its books. It was saved only by virtue of the largest government bailout in history — about $180 billion. The rest of 2008 was a nightmare. We can only hope that it was the bottom of the crisis.

Chapter Six

Asleep on the Beat

As I think about the financial crisis and the events that led up to it, I can't help but shake my head over the role of the Securities and Exchange Commission. Never has one agency done so little to protect so many from so few.

The SEC was created in 1934 in the aftermath of the Crash of 1929 with a mission to regulate the stock market and prevent corporate abuses in the sale of stock and in financial reporting by public companies. In other words, the SEC was the cop on the financial markets beat, charged with protecting investors from unscrupulous brokers and corporate officials. So let's think for a moment about some notable recent examples of bad companies and bad brokers and how well the SEC policed its beat.

We can start with Enron, a colossal fraud perpetrated over a number of years. The SEC completely missed that one. And there was WorldCom, another gigantic fraud that the SEC completely missed. Bernie Madoff ran his gigantic Ponzi scheme for years while the SEC shrugged off warnings from some astute investors as early as 1999 that it was legally impossible for Madoff to make the kinds of profits he reported using the strategies he claimed. It took the collapse of the markets to undermine Madoff's little scheme and awaken the SEC to the fraud. And only when Madoff was finally exposed did the SEC move to shut down another alleged Ponzi scheme, one that was accused of operating right in my back yard. Unfortunately it was too late to save billions of dollars of investors' money.

In February 2009, the SEC shut down Stanford Financial Group and its related entities, which, since 2005, had been operating a Stanford Group Company office in Lafayette, where local investors' losses on so-called certificates of deposit in Antigua-based Stanford International Bank are estimated to be in the hundreds of millions of dollars (potential individual losses to local investors in Lafayette are as high as $27 million). The SEC characterized Stanford's alleged $8 billion Ponzi scheme as "a fraud of shocking magnitude that has spread its tentacles throughout the world." What still has so many people scratching their heads is the fact that whistleblowers had been coming forward for years; there is overwhelming evidence that financial advisers at the company had been reporting their suspicions since at least 2003. The purported returns on the CDs, 3 percent to 4 percent higher than those in the United States, just weren't possible. Everyone knew that. Still, the company pushed its advisers hard to sell the CDs, motivating them with bonuses like BMWs and outrageous commissions, money that was so easy to come by it was eventually nicknamed "bank crack." Stanford financial adviser Leyla Wydler (then Leyla Basagoitia) said she refused to sell the CDs, believing they were too risky, and was promptly fired in 2002. She reported her suspicions that Stanford was running a Ponzi scheme to regulatory watchdogs including the SEC from 2003 to 2004, but her complaints were seemingly ignored.

Just as Stanford Group Company was expanding from Baton Rouge to Lafayette in 2005, two Venezuelans were also alleging in U.S. District Court in Florida that Stanford International Bank knowingly aided and abetted "a classic Ponzi scheme" that targeted Venezuelans, according to a February 2009 report in *The Wall Street Journal*. A year later a former Stanford employee, Lawrence J. DeMaria, filed suit against Stanford in Florida state court, alleging that the company was operating a pyramid scheme, taking new money to its offshore bank, laundering the money, and using the money to finance its growing brokerage business, which did not have any profits of its own. In early 2008, while Stanford was celebrating the opening of its bigger, upscale office in Lafayette's River Ranch, where there is a high concentration of wealth, two of its former financial advisers, Charles Rawl and Mark Tidwell, were making blistering allegations against the company in Texas state court. They said that in the summer of 2006, when the SEC was planning an inspection of the company files, Stanford management ordered the removal or destruction of significant amounts of information from clients' files and also purged data from its computers. They also said Stanford told them not to notify clients who had invested in the CDs about forms they were supposed to submit to the IRS, potentially setting clients up for civil and criminal liability. Reading their allegations now (what they called "illegal and unethical" practices in court documents), and knowing my friends and neighbors were investing in these bogus CDs throughout 2008 when there was ample evidence for the SEC to stop Stanford, is hard to swallow.

Why did the SEC allow this alleged $8 billion Ponzi scheme to go on for so long? That's what 18 Lafayette area investors want to know. To find out, they've hired Edward Gonzales, a Baton Rouge attorney and former federal prosecutor in the Middle District of Louisiana for more than a decade, to investigate the SEC's role.

I would love dearly to blame the entire financial collapse that began in 2008 on the SEC but I can't do that because the agency didn't have the authority to regulate the derivatives that were at the heart of the problem. And the agency didn't try very hard to get that authority. Even if it had obtained the authority, I can only speculate that the SEC would have botched that, too.

Don't get me wrong. I don't mean to imply that the SEC has just stood around on the street corner twiddling its thumbs and doing nothing while crime was busting out all around it. That would be unfair. So let me tell you a little bit about what the SEC was doing all this time. For one thing, it was trying to regulate the banking industry, especially smaller banks, even though they were already pretty heavily regulated and weren't even doing anything wrong. (Unless you listen to the SEC, which ran around accusing a lot of small banks of "manipulating earnings" and then fining them.) By law, banks are required to keep a certain amount of money in what's called a reserve for loan losses. This is money a bank puts aside to cover losses that might happen in future years if, for example, a recession occurs and a lot of borrowers wind up defaulting. Because the banker is trying to predict the future out several years, the amount that goes into the loan loss reserve can vary quite a bit. It's a judgment call. And because the money that is put into the loan loss reserve isn't counted as profit in the bank's quarterly and annual financial statements, the temptation, as you might suspect, is not to put a whole lot of money in the reserve. Better for the bank and for its shareholders if you can report fatter profits rather than fatter loan loss reserves. Nevertheless, the SEC believed that banks had decided to hide profits by putting more money in the loan loss reserves than they needed to. The SEC figured that whenever times got tough and profits were falling, the banks would then bring some of that money out of the reserve to prop up profits. It was, the SEC said, a big scheme to confuse investors about the banks' real profitability. So while Enron and WorldCom burned, the SEC attacked banks for doing something that few bankers in their right mind would do.

Of course, the SEC was embarrassed by the failures of Enron and WorldCom. When the finger-pointing began, the head of the SEC, William Donaldson, immediately started whining about not having enough funds and people to do the job properly. What did Congress do? It gave him more people and money, never bothering to ask if perhaps there was another reason that the agency had missed Enron and WorldCom. So now the SEC had to come up with something to do with all that money and people, and the answer in 2002 was a law called Sarbanes-Oxley, named after Sen. Paul Sarbanes, a Maryland

Democrat, and Rep. Michael Oxley, an Ohio Republican. On the surface, the law looks fairly simple: It requires the chief executive officer and the chief financial officer of every public company, along with the company's outside auditor, to swear, under penalty of law, that the company's financial results are accurate and proper. In essence, the law requires companies to police themselves, thus letting the SEC off the hook to some extent. Very clever.

But Sarbanes-Oxley, or SOX as it is commonly called, has proven to be one of the worst pieces of legislation ever passed, at least for small businesses. The amount of detail it requires is extraordinary. Big companies and big auditing firms have hundreds, if not thousands, of people engaged in accounting and finance work and highly sophisticated software and hardware to process all the data. It's estimated that the additional cost of complying with SOX is less than one one-hundredth of a big company's overall cost of doing business. But small companies like MidSouth Bank don't have legions of people laboring in accounting and finance, and we don't have huge computer systems and the requisite software to track and categorize all sorts of data. Complying with SOX increases the costs incurred by a small business by 8 percent or even more. To put it in more human terms, Sarbanes-Oxley is like a new income tax that requires the multimillionaire to pay $10 more in taxes while a worker earning $50,000 a year has his tax bill increased by $1,000.

In 2004, the SEC invited me to serve on a study group investigating the impact of Sarbanes-Oxley. Along with some other members who were, like me, heads of small businesses, I tried hard to make two points: first, that Sarbanes-Oxley was a huge problem for small businesses and second, that the consequences of a small business failing would be nothing compared to the scale of an Enron or WorldCom. We urged the SEC to focus its attention on the big companies that had the potential to do real harm to the economy or to hundreds of thousands of investors rather than burden small companies with all that paperwork. But the SEC wasn't much interested in what we had to say and, once again, the big boys prevailed.

Did Sarbanes-Oxley contribute to the global financial crisis? Not really. But neither did it do what it was supposed to do. Right up until the crisis exploded in 2008, all the CEOs and CFOs at places like Merrill Lynch, Bear Stearns, Lehman Brothers, Citigroup, and AIG put their signatures on the required forms swearing that their financial statements were accurate. And now we know, of course, that these statements were untrue. And I still haven't heard of any of those people being charged by the SEC with a violation of Sarbanes-Oxley. So much for your friendly cop on the beat.

Federal Reserve Chairman Alan Greenspan was convinced that bigger was better and didn't want to hear advice from small-town bankers — when it was correct!

Rep. Hank Johnson of Georgia was chairman of the House Judiciary subcommittee that invited me to testify on too-big-to-fail institutions in March 2009.

I led a delegation from the Independent Community Bankers of America in 2003 to try to impress on Senate Majority Leader Bill Frist the growing danger of big banks and their risky behavior.

I believed it was particularly important for regulators like Don Powell, chairman of the Federal Deposit Insurance Corporation when this photo was taken in 2002, to understand the growing problems with big banks.

My testimony in March 2009 before Illinois Rep. Luis Gutiérrez's subcommittee on financial institutions developed into the Twenty Recommendations for the future in Chapter 14.

In 2003, I made a special effort to be sure that John Korsmo, chairman of the Federal Housing Finance Board, understood the risks of letting the Chicago office get into the mortgage business.

My fellow Cajun, Sen. John Breaux (now retired), was a "go to" guy in D.C. and a friend of the Independent Community Bankers of America.

In January and February of 2009, when the big banks were near collapse and refusing to lend, I did a series of town hall meetings in communities MidSouth Bank serves to tell businesspeople we had money to lend and were eager to do business.

Chapter Seven

Triple A, All Day, Every Day

'These errors make us look either incompetent
at credit analysis or like we sold our soul
to the devil for revenue, or a little bit of both.'

— A Moody's Investors Service managing director
responding to an internal survey in 2007,
as reported by *The New York Times* in 2008.

A cozy — yet conflicted — relationship has existed for years between the big banks and brokerage firms and the nation's three big debt ratings agencies: Moody's, Standard & Poor's, and Fitch Ratings.

If you've ever bought a corporate bond for your retirement or investment portfolio you're probably familiar with the ratings agencies and their somewhat arcane methods of evaluating the safety of a bond. I'll use Standard & Poor's ratings system as an example. If a big, very profitable company in a lucrative industry issues a bond, S&P's analysts might give it their highest rating: AAA. That means the company should be able to pay the interest and return the principal on the bond without any problems. A bond issued by a company that is making money but already has some outstanding debt might get a rating of AA, A, or BBB, which means there are some economic circumstances that could affect the company's ability to pay interest and repay the principal. Bonds issued by companies that are even more vulnerable to economic or financial problems that might affect their ability to pay interest or repay the principal are deemed "Non-investment Grade" and get ratings of BB, B, CCC, CC, or C. These bonds aren't called "junk bonds" for nothing. There's a real risk you might not get your money back from those companies. Moody's uses a somewhat similar system with ratings like Aaa on down to Baa1; Ba3 right through Caa1; Caa2 and ending at C. Why they can't use a simpler system such as one-star, two-star, etc., is beyond me, but that's how it works.

Obviously if you want to invest in a safe bond you would want it to carry a AAA rating. But remember, the safer a bond is considered, the lower the interest rate it pays. So if you want a little extra yield from your bond investments you might settle for bonds rated AA, A, or even B. You probably should use only your "play money" to invest (gamble) on junk bonds.

The point is for years investors have relied on the ratings agencies' smart analysts to keep an eagle eye on the bond market and make sure investors know what they're getting when they buy a bond. And for a long time that was a very good system. Big investors paid the agencies to analyze bonds and tell them how safe they were. Sure, a company might not like it when the agencies rated the company's bonds at BB because it meant the company would have to pay bond investors a higher interest rate, but there wasn't much the company could do about it. The Securities and Exchange Commission was so impressed by the analytical skills and unbiased ratings that in 1975 it essentially anointed them as the official arbiters of credit analysis.

Ironically, the SEC's approval came at around the same time the ratings agencies figured out they could make more money if instead of being paid by investors to rate a bond, they charged the issuer of the bond a fee to rate it. After all, given the SEC's imprimatur, any company that wanted to issue a bond had to get it rated. Of course it was pretty easy to see that such an arrangement created a conflict of interest. If you pay someone to rate your product, chances are you'll get a pretty good rating. We learned just how great that conflict of interest can be when Enron and WorldCom both collapsed. The rating agencies had put very high ratings on the bonds issued by both companies. When they collapsed it became very clear that they were massive frauds and the sharp-eyed analysts at the agencies had missed or ignored that little fact. Still, nothing was really done about the situation, and the agencies kept collecting fees from companies to rate their bonds.

Back in the old days, rating bonds wasn't a terribly complicated business. The analysts would look at the issuer's finances, examine the industry's vulnerability to an economic slump, and make a decision. But then came securitization, which we've talked about in previous chapters. You'll recall that it's the process in which a bank or mortgage broker packages up lots of loans and sells that package as a bond. Securitization made it a bit more difficult for the analysts at the agencies to evaluate how safe a bond was. After all, if the bond consisted of 1,000 mortgages, how was the agency going to examine each one of those borrowers to judge the risk of default? The answer, basically, was that the agencies took the word of the bank or broker that the homeowners had made a down payment, that their income was sufficient to make the mortgage payments, and that the house they bought was appraised properly. That required a degree of trust in the banks' lending standards, but because the Wall Street banks were paying the ratings fee it wasn't a big stretch for the agencies to trust them.

Then came collateralized debt obligations and credit default swaps. They, too, were bonds, but they were like no bonds anyone had seen before. Made up as they were of many different parts and pieces carved out of a huge pile of mortgages, it became even more difficult to judge the underlying safety of those packages. Because it was so difficult, the ratings agencies charged much higher fees to analyze a CDO or CDS. Recall, too, that the banks and mortgage brokers were getting a lot less careful about their lending standards. If they intended to simply bundle up the mortgage and sell it to someone else to carve up into a CDO, what difference did it make to them if the borrower took out a "no-doc" loan with nothing down?

So here's the situation in about 2006: Everybody wants to own real estate because prices are rocketing higher and always will. Buy that condo today, flip it tomorrow. Lenders are falling all over themselves to make the American Dream of homeownership come true for everyone, no matter their income or assets. And the whiz kids are taking all those mortgages and creating "synthetic derivatives" and asking the ratings agencies to give those weird instruments a good rating. Billions of dollars worth of CDOs were rated AAA. But those CDOs that were rated AAA also happened to pay a very high rate of interest. Investors loved them: a supposedly safe bond that paid like a junk bond.

It was so obvious that something was wrong. Triple-A rated debt simply shouldn't pay a high interest rate. Now we know that either the ratings agencies were clueless or they failed their responsibilities to the investment community by allowing Wall Street and the big banks to sell investors all over the world what have come to be called "toxic assets." When the borrowers whose mortgages underlay the CDOs defaulted, the value of the CDOs plunged. I say the value plunged, but the reality was nobody had any idea what they were worth because suddenly nobody wanted to own one and there was no market mechanism to price them. And that's how we got ourselves into a global financial crisis.

Were the ratings agencies to blame? Certainly they don't bear the entire blame for the global financial crisis. But their performance obviously leaves a lot to be desired.

Chapter Eight

From Pay Day to Doomsday

There was a song Frank Sinatra made popular in the 1960s called "It Was A Very Good Year," and its title sums up life for the big banks and brokerages in 2006. That was the year when Goldman Sachs paid more than 50 of its people more than $20 million each. That was the year when Merrill Lynch paid its chief executive, Stanley O'Neal, $46 million. And the list can go on and on and on: Charles Prince at CitiGroup, Richard Fuld at Lehman Brothers, James Cayne at Bear Stearns, Ken Lewis at Bank of America. All of them and many of the people below them involved in packaging and selling derivatives based on home mortgages earned millions each in bonuses that reflected the huge profits their institutions were making.

That kind of bonus pay had been going on for years, and the people who reaped those lavish rewards did their part to fuel America's consumer economy. They bought giant houses and expensive sports cars, threw lavish dinners and parties, and engaged in every other form of conspicuous consumption they could think of. And they were certain they deserved every penny based on the profits their firms were minting.

The only problem was that there really weren't any huge profits. The year 2006 was the last full year before the toxic nature of mortgage derivatives began to become evident and the global financial system began to implode. Now, you and I are paying a portion of our income taxes to try to save those same firms, many of which have reported losses far in excess of the profits they claimed to have earned in the years leading up to the disaster. The taxpayer bill will run into billions of dollars, and our nation will be paying that tab for years to come.

But what about those executives and traders who got those big bonuses while their practices got us into this fix? Shouldn't they be repaying the companies — so that we don't have to bail them out! — because they really didn't produce any profits at all?

Unfortunately, it doesn't work that way. They aren't giving back their bonuses. You see, the big banks want a one-way ticket. They'll take the bonuses when the times seem good, but they want us to swallow the losses when their risky deals blow up. Even when some of the most richly rewarded CEOs get fired for being incompetent, they still walk away with huge payouts. Stanley O'Neal, the man who wrecked Merrill Lynch, was awarded an exit package worth $161 million when the board tossed him out.

Obviously, there's something wrong with these kinds of pay packages, and it isn't hard to see what it is. Banks and brokerages pay their people for short-term results even though those results carry with them long-term ramifications. The traders and bankers went on a six-year binge and got rewarded each year for their efforts. When it all exploded in the seventh year, they just shrugged and began looking for ways to get the government to bail out their firms so they could collect some more bonuses. In a situation like that there is just too much incentive to take extraordinary risks so you can collect your fat bonus before the products you created and sold blow up. And that is exactly what happened.

Now that we, the taxpayers, are bailing them out, they still want bonuses. Before he was kicked out as head of Merrill Lynch, John Thain, who indulged in $1.2 million in office renovations in 2008 as he was preparing to slash jobs, argued that Merrill should be allowed to divert some of the taxpayer dollars that were saving it from destruction to pay bonuses in order to reward and retain talent. I have a hard time thinking of people who nearly wrecked our economy as particularly talented.

If you think about the pay situation on Wall Street and at the big banks you can get a little angry. After all, entrepreneurs who go out and start businesses take huge risks. Sure, some of them win big time like Steve Jobs at Apple or Bill Gates at Microsoft. But many more don't make it so big and more than a few fail outright. But big-time bankers? Heads they win, tails we lose. Robert Rubin, the former U.S. Treasury Secretary and vice chairman of Citigroup, was paid close to $115 million for his "work" at Citigroup, and now you and I are paying for the bets he made that he lost.

Makes you a little sick, doesn't it?

Part III
The Hall of Shame

Chapter Nine

SEND IN THE MARINE!

I f America's big banks are really "too big to fail," there's one guy who shoulders a lot of the blame: Hugh McColl Jr. A true pioneer in the banking industry, McColl skirted the edges of the law and played a masterful strategic game against government regulators to turn a middling bank in North Carolina into one of the nation's biggest financial institutions.

McColl came from a family with a long tradition of banking in South Carolina. But before he could follow his forefathers' footsteps into banking, the onset of the Great Depression forced his father to sell the family-owned Bank of Marlboro and become a cotton merchant. It was a good business and Hugh was the beneficiary of his daddy's money. He loved sports and having a good time. Academics, not so much. Mostly, he was a C student except for As in accounting, math, and finance — a sign of things to come.

After college McColl joined the U.S. Marines Corps. He was a marine for only two years, but the esprit de corps and ethos of the organization would stay with him forever. After his tour of duty, he returned to South Carolina, confident he would go into his father's cotton business. But his father had other ideas. There was no room in the cotton business, he told his son, but he did know about an opportunity to get into banking. McColl wound up starting as a trainee for American Commercial Bank in Charlotte, N.C. Not long afterward, American Commercial merged with Security National Bank in Greensboro to become North Carolina National Bank.

By all accounts McColl was a diligent banker. But he applied the Marine Corps approach to everything: Charge! Not only was he good at making loans — he traveled all over the Southeast persuading companies to borrow money from North Carolina National Bank, later renamed NCNB — but he also had a knack for handling loans that went bad, a skill that would serve him well later. During the recession in the mid 1970s, NCNB was facing some $28 million in bad loans. McColl went to work on the customers who weren't paying, and by the time he was finished that potential $28 million had been worked down to just $2 million.

His hard work and obvious executive skills propelled McColl up the executive ranks of NCNB. His ambition was reflected not just in his swift promotions, but also in his ideas about expanding NCNB's territory. Even before he took the reins of NCNB, McColl was thinking about ways his bank could grow outside of North Carolina. Granted, it was already doing business throughout the Southeast, but McColl didn't want to jet into town and do business out of a hotel room. He wanted NCNB to have a brick-and-mortar presence and the place he wanted to start that expansion was the booming

Florida market. In 1982 it was illegal to branch across state lines. But that didn't stop McColl. He had NCNB buy Trust Company of Florida and convert it into a bank. It wasn't storming the beaches in Marine style, but his backdoor approach got the job done.

When McColl was named chairman and chief executive in 1983, he had been preparing for years to fight a war for banking dominance in the United States. As I watched him carry out his campaign of one acquisition after another to build a coast-to-coast banking empire, I saw that his strategy emulated the Marines in the Pacific during World War II when they went "island hopping," staging bloody amphibious landings to capture one island after another as they marched toward Japan. Like them, McColl would capture one bank at a time, steadily advancing across the United States.

In 1988, McColl staged a real coup when he managed to buy First RepublicBank Corporation of Texas after it failed and was being essentially auctioned off by the Federal Deposit Insurance Corporation. There was no backdoor maneuvering for that one; it was a frontal assault. McColl knew the FDIC was considering awarding the Texas bank to one of a number of ambitious national banks. So in an operation reminiscent of a Marines invasion, he sent 250 of his top bankers to Texas, each with orders to set up shop in a hotel near a FirstRepublic branch bank or subsidiaries. If NCNB won, McColl wanted to have his people walking into the newly acquired branches within minutes of the announcement. Of course word got around about what was happening, and the fact that McColl was willing to spend so much money just to be prepared probably convinced the FDIC that NCNB should get the nod. It did, and it even got a sweet tax deal from the Internal Revenue Service that helped make the deal a winner. (Big bankers rant and rave about government interference but don't hesitate to grab any benefit the government offers!) Suddenly, McColl's bank had grown to $60 billion in assets.

His next target was Atlanta-based C&S/Sovran. That one was fairly easy, the result of negotiations between McColl and C&S's chairman, Bennett Brown. The agreement they signed created NationsBank, the nation's third-largest bank, with assets of $119 billion and 59,000 employees working in 2,000 branches. The name change is symbolic of McColl's ego and ambition. Even though few people remembered that NCNB stood for North Carolina National Bank, he wanted everything to be bigger and grander. His entire strategy was about growth. If you were a loan officer, you made money not by bringing in profitable loans, but by bringing in big loans.

McColl also was a master of the political game. While building NCNB, he was ingratiating himself with many political figures, among them the young governor of Arkansas, Bill Clinton. When Clinton was elected president, McColl had ready entree to the White House, Treasury, and Federal Reserve. He was Clinton's favorite banker, and in 1994 the relationship paid off: Under McColl's guidance the White House and the Congress passed the Interstate Banking and Branching Act. That opened the legal door to the capstone of McColl's career in April 1998 when NationsBank merged with San Francisco-based BankAmerican to become Bank of America with headquarters in Charlotte.

With the conclusion of that deal McColl had seen his bank grow from $12 billion in assets and 7,600 employees to an institution with assets of $642 billion and 149,000 employees. He retired in 1999, a year in which he was paid $49 million.

There's no denying McColl's energy, drive, ambition and smarts. But his career wasn't without its problems. McColl was blunt spoken and had little regard for the traditions of the banks he took over. Some in the media labeled him the George Patton of banking, a reference to the hard-nosed World War II general. And in his constant quest for growth, McColl sometimes overlooked things like credit quality.

Throughout my career I could see that McColl never built a bank the old-fashioned way: open an office, hire some good people, and build a quality institution. Instead, all his deals were of a kind: Buy the franchise, then destroy the community banks that had been built over many years, and then move on to the next conquest. He was a lot like General William Tecumseh Sherman, who laid waste to the South during the Civil War.

But I have to give McColl credit, too, because he knew all along that the bank had become too big for one man to manage and he brought in a lot of smart people to help him. Ken Lewis, a longtime protégé, took over after McColl retired and seemed to be doing a decent job. Still, Bank of America was "too big to fail," and when the crunch came, Lewis made a fatal mistake: His ego and the continuing urge to get bigger prompted him to "rescue" Merrill Lynch, which was on the edge of collapse in December 2008, without digging deeply enough to see how badly injured Merrill was. Allegations of wrongdoing would haunt the merger as well. Lawsuits filed by several state attorneys general accused Bank of America of authorizing as much as $5.8 billion in end-of-year bonuses to Merrill executives, but failing to disclose the payments before the merger vote. Within weeks Merrill's problems were crashing around Lewis' head, and Bank of America had joined the list of "zombie" banks, too big to fail, but failing nevertheless. In the end, the ill-fated Merrill deal would be Lewis' downfall: On Sept. 30, 2009, the embattled chief executive told board members he would take early retirement.

Was it McColl's fault that Bank of America became "too big to fail?" Absolutely. He was the father of this crisis, the most powerful banker in America who, by force of will, made other bankers like Sandy Weill play the game of "too big to fail." But he can't shoulder all the blame. He had plenty of helpers in the form of regulators who let him grow and competitors who tried to keep up by running around madly buying banks to grow their own empires.

Chapter Ten

THE PRINCE OF DARKNESS

I never begrudge people with ambition for success, unless their ambition threatens everyone else's success. Sanford Weill, better known as Sandy, is perhaps the most ambitious man I've ever seen short of some candidates for president of the United States. Along with Alan Greenspan, the former Federal Reserve chairman, Sandy Weill — I call him "The Prince of Darkness" — bears much of the burden for the global economic collapse that inflicted so much damage.

Weill's career is a classic tale of the striver, the underdog always pushing for success and adulation. After a lackluster college career he sought work in 1955 as a broker on Wall Street, but was firmly turned down by the big investment banks. He did, however, manage to land a job as a lowly runner for Bear Stearns. He was paid only $35 a week, but the job carrying documents to and from various Wall Street firms and the New York Stock Exchange introduced him to the intricacies of the financial industry. Gradually, he worked himself up the ladder in Bear Stearns' back office, where all the paperwork was done. Like my early experience in Morgan City learning the loan business, Weill got a very valuable education in how securities firms worked. It wasn't a glamorous job like being a broker — a job he eventually won after earning his license — but it was infinitely more important in shaping Weill's career.

After gaining more experience at Bear Stearns, Weill set up his own firm with several partners. The firm did well, mostly because the market was rising through the 1960s. In fact, Wall Street was generating so much business that the back offices of the big firms couldn't keep up with all the paperwork. Stock certificates and bonds were getting lost, trades weren't being executed correctly and there was much concern about how it would all end. That concern came to a head in 1970 when the market tanked and lots of brokerage firms were in big trouble. But not Weill's firm. He knew how to run a back office and how to get business done. So when the big brokerage firm of Mc-Donnell & Co. announced it was closing in 1970, the New York Stock Exchange let Weill's firm buy McDonnell's Beverly Hills office for pennies on the dollar. Then another old-line prestigious firm, Hayden Stone & Co., came close to failure, and this time the New York Stock Exchange sought out Weill to "rescue" Hayden Stone by buying it for almost nothing. Suddenly the mouse had swallowed the elephant, and Weill was becoming something of a celebrity on Wall Street for his back-office acumen.

Weill continued to build a financial empire over the next several years through canny acquisitions and aggressive management. But in 1981 the financial world changed radically almost overnight when Prudential Insurance Corp. announced it was buying Bache Halsey Stuart Shields, a securities firm.

That was a wake-up call for Weill. If huge players like Prudential began getting into the securities business, the existing brokerage firms would be hard-pressed to compete. Weill knew he had to hook up with a big financial firm himself or face destructive competition from those who did. Uncharacteristically he did a deal in which he sold his firm rather than buy another company. The deal with American Express in 1981 meant he was no longer the head dog, and he couldn't stand that. When he parted ways with American Express it looked as if Weill's meteoric career in finance had flamed out for good.

But just a few years later Weill was back, this time as head of a Baltimore-based company called Commercial Credit Corp. Basically, it was a forerunner of today's subprime lenders, making loans to customers who couldn't borrow money from real banks and charging them very high interest rates. I have to admit that it seemed Weill did a very good job of managing Commercial Credit, which is unusual among people whose main aim is to build an empire through acquisitions. Nevertheless he remained hell bent on building that empire. Over the years he engineered the acquisition of Primerica and its two important subsidiaries, the big brokerage firm Smith Barney and the insurance company A.L. Williams. And in 1992 when Hurricane Andrew's wide swath of destruction in south Florida threatened to sink Travelers Insurance, Weill bought that, too, taking Travelers' name for his steadily growing company and adopting the insurance company's iconic red umbrella as his corporate symbol.

By that time Weill had firmly established his reputation as a master of the financial industry, both in terms of managing companies and building an empire. Any reasonable person would have been satisfied, but Weill wasn't reasonable. He wanted more. He decided that he wanted to own a bank, and not just any bank. He wanted the biggest and the best: Citicorp. In February 1998, Weill proposed to John Reed, the CEO of Citicorp, that they merge Travelers and Citi. Weill and Reed would serve as co-chairmen of the behemoth financial services company. There was, of course, a problem: such a merger was illegal on the face of it because it violated the Glass-Steagall Act, a law passed during the Great Depression that forbade a commercial bank (Citi) from owning or being owned by an investment bank (Travelers and its Smith Barney subsidiary). Congress isn't always the brightest group of people on the face of the earth, but legislators passed Glass-Steagall for a very good reason: The kinds of dealings it forbade were partly responsible for the devastation wrought by the Great Depression. "Never again," they said. But those Depression-era congressmen didn't reckon with Sandy Weill, whose machinations to get Glass-Steagall repealed played a big role in setting up the crisis afflicting us today. Back in 2000 Weill was hailed as a visionary and dealmaker par excellence. Today, he is persona non grata among my many friends in the banking industry who have seen their once-cherished industry brought to its knees by the multiple failures of Weill and his lieutenants and competitors to take care that banking and bankers remain the souls of probity and trust.

I still wonder what was going through John Reed's mind when he allowed Sandy Weill to persuade him to merge Citicorp with Travelers. Although Reed hadn't much use for us small-town bankers, I nevertheless thought he was an intelligent man. Merging your company with one run by Weill is something akin to marrying a rattlesnake. You're going to be a lot worse off than if you stayed single. The fact that the merger was illegal didn't seem to bother Reed nor anyone in government. Weill assured Reed that the law would be changed after they announced their planned merger. President Clinton, of course, didn't get very involved: He had more pressing matters on his hands in the form of a young intern, Monica Lewinsky, who had befriended him. But Weill and Reed had other powerful allies in the government in the form of Alan Greenspan, chairman of the Federal Reserve; Treasury Secretary Robert Rubin, himself a former investment banker; and Larry Summers, who was Deputy Treasury Secretary and now heads President Obama's National Economic Council. They all thought it was a fine idea to get rid of Glass-Steagall and let banks cozy up to investment firms and insurance companies.

Now if you think about it, what business are investment firms and insurance companies really in? It's financial risk. They're always running around taking risks. I know that it takes risks to get rewards, and it's fine if they want to do that. But when you hook a bank up to an investment firm or an insurance company, how do you keep the traders and insurance brokers who are taking those big risks from tapping the money that's supposedly sitting safely in the vaults? Apparently that question either didn't come up or the smart guys in Washington thought they had an answer. In any case, Greenspan went before Congress to persuade your elected representatives to repeal Glass-Steagall. Financial deregulation was the watchword of the day, and Greenspan made his case: bigger is better and the biggest is best. When Congress repealed Glass-Steagall in 1999, the only question in some peoples' minds was whether the relatively conservative Citibank culture or the gun-slinging culture of Travelers would prevail. I didn't need to ask; I knew the answer. Sure enough, within a year Weill had engineered the ouster of Reed, his co-chairman of the renamed Citigroup, and the cowboys were in charge. Sandy Weill, the Prince of Darkness, had created the Death Star of financial firms, one that would carry our nation's economy into ruin within the next several years. I admire cowboys for winning the Wild West, but they have no place in charge of the nation's biggest banks, as recent events have since proven very clearly.

Once he had control of Citigroup, Weill set out to change the way the company did business. He had ousted Reed and made Robert Rubin, the former Treasury Secretary, chairman of the company's executive committee with a salary in the millions. In February 2000, soon after Weill forced Reed out, I was testifying before a large panel in front of the House Banking Committee, run that day by Rep. Richard Baker of Louisiana, on the future of Fannie Mae and Freddie Mac. This was one of the first hearings on the mortgage companies and some of the potential problems they were having. But we got off that subject pretty quickly when the consumer protection people, who were also testifying, kept bringing up Citigroup's efforts to buy Associates First Capital from Ford Motor Co. Associates was the kind of business that was close to Weill's heart: making loans to people who could not get bank loans from a place like MidSouth and charging them very high rates. But the consumer group kept saying that this was one of the largest predatory lenders in America. Citigroup continued to deny it at the hearing, and the members of Congress pushed the Fed to hold up the application until the situation could be clarified. No thanks, Greenspan said, and Citigroup got the go-ahead and moved quickly to close the deal. Even though Citigroup was known to be a large subprime mortgage operator, the Federal Reserve chose to ignore that fact. But the Federal Trade Commission picked up the ball and started looking into Citigroup's single premium insurance product that it was adding to the subprime loans, greatly increasing the cost to poor borrowers. In 2002 Citigroup came to an agreement with the FTC and paid a fine of $200 million for this practice. Yet all the while the Federal Reserve under Greenspan was still pushing for them to bring more products to the market and to expand Citigroup's banking dominance.

Once he had amassed all that financial clout, Weill put Citigroup on the path that led to disaster. Next thing we knew Citigroup was down in Houston, Texas, doing deals with a company called Enron, formerly Houston Natural Gas. Houston Natural Gas had been a sleepy supplier of natural gas to businesses and consumers. But when Kenneth Lay ("Kenny Boy" to his pal President George W. Bush) took over shortly after supporting Bush in 1998, he renamed it Enron and hired one of McKinsey & Co.'s brightest, a fellow named Jeff Skilling, as CFO. Skilling was a master of "off-balance sheet transactions" that, although risky, didn't appear on the company's books and thus didn't appear to auditors and others, including

Citigroup bankers, to be any problem.

Doing things off the books is never a good way to do business, especially for a public company. The whole point of being "public" is to provide potential shareholders with transparency into how you run your business. But Congress didn't seem to worry about that when it passed legislation in 2000 that permitted the widespread use of such off-the-books deals. It didn't hurt, of course, that Sen. Phil Gramm of Texas, who pushed for the deregulation that allowed it, had his wife Wendy, supposedly an "expert" on oil and gas futures, sitting on Enron's board as chairwoman of its audit committee. Even as Citigroup was getting into bed with Enron, it was also carrying on a torrid financial affair with another company called WorldCom. WorldCom, run by a former high school gym teacher named Bernard Ebbers and headquartered in Jackson, Miss., was cutting a huge swath through the telecom business. Citigroup's chief telecom analyst, Jack Grubman, couldn't praise WorldCom's prospects loudly enough in public, even though he was quietly telling close associates the company was a failure waiting to happen. In exchange for his vociferous praise of WorldCom, Grubman enlisted Weill's aid in getting the Grubman kids into elite New York schools.

You know the rest. Both Enron and WorldCom collapsed, despite Robert Rubin's efforts to persuade the Bush administration to bail out Enron. The result was massive shareholder lawsuits against Citigroup, an investigation of the bank by Attorney General Eliot Spitzer of New York and an SEC sanction barring Grubman from the securities business. It cost Citigroup a few billion dollars to settle the suits, and any right-minded person would figure that the SEC, Congress, and the Fed would crack down on such practices. Well, they said they did, but the results didn't really fix anything and cost my bank and hundreds more millions of dollars meeting the new requirements that the big banks, as it turned out, just ignored. We had done nothing wrong, yet we were being penalized.

Enron and WorldCom were just the beginning of Citigroup's woes under Weill and then his chosen heir, Chuck Prince. Just as I knew would happen, Citigroup's gunslingers plunged deeper and deeper into the subprime loan market and into the esoteric business of trading derivatives. Citigroup, of course, was no different from other big banks and investment firms like Merrill Lynch, AIG, Bank of America, Lehman Brothers, and Bear Stearns. All those and many more were guilty of taking on too much risk in an effort to make money. But I still think that if Weill hadn't let his greed and determination get the best of him we would still be operating under the restrictions of Glass-Steagall. I often wonder about how much less pain we would have suffered in the economic crisis if Weill's ambitions had been checked.

Chapter Eleven

THE EMPEROR OF AMERICA

J
ust as the wise congressmen who passed the Glass-Steagall Act amid the economic wreckage of the Great Depression couldn't anticipate that an egomaniac like Sandy Weill would undo their handiwork decades later, they also could not have foreseen that he would be aided and abetted by the person most responsible for the sanctity and safety of the nation's banks, the head of the Federal Reserve. Alan Greenspan, a mumble-mouthed economist, was appointed Federal Reserve Chairman in 1987 by Ronald Reagan, perhaps one of the most economically clueless presidents the United States has ever had. The fact is very few presidents have the background or the interest to craft their own economic policy. Usually they turn that job over to the Secretary of the Treasury, which makes that a powerful and important position. Under Reagan, that job was held by Donald Regan, former CEO of Merrill Lynch. Regan, like most Wall Street executives, advocated giving the markets free rein, and it wasn't any accident that when President Reagan had a chance to appoint a new chairman of the Federal Reserve Board — another pow-

erful and important economic job — Donald Regan pushed Alan Greenspan as the leading candidate. Greenspan went on to head the Fed for 19 years under four presidents: Ronald Reagan, George Bush, Bill Clinton, and George W. Bush. He used his power to exercise unprecedented and unchecked influence over the American economy. Given his long tenure and his immense power with no accountability, I think of Alan Greenspan as the Emperor of America. Essentially, he was America's economic dictator.

Like any dictator, Greenspan kept an iron grip on the people under him. He wanted executives of big banks to serve on the Fed because they shared his view that bigger is always better in banking. He didn't want to hear any other point of view. His obsession with controlling the members of the Fed was evident in 2001 when a group of congressmen and some senators were pushing for a young North Dakota banker named Terry Jorde to be appointed to the Fed. Jorde, who would later go on to become chairman of the Independent Community Bankers of America and prove herself as an able executive and would have been an outstanding addition to the Fed. But Greenspan, according to press accounts at the time, lobbied heavily with President George W. Bush to block the nomination, and Jorde never made it. That was a true loss to the American people.

Greenspan also exhibited his penchant for big bankers in the way he controlled the Federal Advisory Council. You've probably never heard of the Federal Advisory Council, and that isn't an accident. Set up when the Federal Reserve was created in 1913, the FAC is a group of 12 bankers, one from each of the Federal Reserve districts, who meet periodically in private to give the Fed their views of what is happening in the economy and what policies the Fed should adopt. Their conferences are not subject to open meetings laws and the members of the FAC are well disciplined. They don't leak to the press because they know they'll lose their position on the FAC if the source is ever discovered. Needless to say, the leaders of small banks seldom get the coveted invitation to join the FAC, and thus their valuable views, drawn from close associations in the communities they serve, are seldom heard in the secret councils of economic power. That's the sole province of the big bankers. Talk about foxes guarding the hen house!

Greenspan left the job in 2006, just before everything began to unravel. Since then he has claimed he has no responsibility for the economic carnage that swept the globe. Yet there are plenty of critics, including Nobel Prize-winning economist Paul Krugman, who pin most of the blame for the crisis squarely on Greenspan. Let me tell you how I see it and then you can decide.

From my point of view there were several things that combined over the years to lead us into the economic collapse: market bubbles first in the form of technology in the late 1990s and then housing in the years leading up to 2006; financial institutions that were allowed to become too big to fail; and, finally, a serious lack of regulation. As far as I know Greenspan had a hand in all three. Apparently he grew up believing that government was an evil influence that merely got in the way of markets doing their thing for the betterment of society, or at least that part of society that had a lot of money. He had an unshakeable faith that the leaders of the nation's largest financial institutions could be trusted to act responsibly and thus there was no need to regulate them.

Greenspan's tenure as chairman of the Fed got off to what seemed to be a good start. When the stock market crashed in October 1987, just a few months after he took the reins, Greenspan announced that the Fed was prepared to flood the economy with money to prevent an economic debacle. His reassurances seemed to work since things returned to normal fairly quickly. But we now know that the stock market crash of 1987 had nothing to do with the fundamental soundness of the economy, which would have gone along just fine without Greenspan's reassurances. Nevertheless, he impressed a lot of people back then, including members of Congress. Anytime he would testify he would be treated with reverence and respect. He spoke in economic jargon that I know very few congressmen understood — if, indeed, Greenspan understood it himself — but they were too awestruck to question him about what he was saying lest they reveal their own lack of understanding about economics.

So here was this guy who was the head regulator of the U.S. banking system and, therefore, the de facto head regulator of the global banking system, and he was a huge fan of deregulation. It was pretty obvious to me from the get-go that Alan Greenspan had never met a big-time banker who he didn't like and had never met a small-time banker who he did like. With his deregulatory mindset he went about the business of making it easier and easier for his beloved big bankers to expand their franchises and become even bigger while making it more and more difficult for small banks to thrive and prosper. He never said it in so many words, but if small banks were pressed hard enough, he knew they would simply sell themselves to the big banks.

Now I'm not a confrontational person, but it was so obvious what Greenspan was doing that I called him on it one day. A group of us community bankers had set up a meeting at the Fed office in Washington in the early 2000s to talk about raising deposit insurance from $100,000 to $150,000 or $200,000. Greenspan didn't like the idea because it would help small banks retain customers, but of course he couldn't say that to us. So he said he opposed it on the grounds that providing that much deposit insurance would be a threat to the U.S. Treasury. The guy simply had no shame. He had already persuaded Congress to repeal Glass-Steagall and was letting the big banks run wild across the country, snapping up everything they could and becoming too big to fail and he sat there and told us with a straight face that increasing the protections for ordinary citizens with checking accounts and savings accounts was going to bankrupt the U.S. Treasury. Then he started to lecture me, telling me that I didn't understand that the root cause of the widespread bank and thrift failures in the 1980s was an increase in deposit insurance from $40,000 to $100,000. That's when I interrupted him, and everyone in the room kind of gasped. No one interrupts the Chairman of the Federal Reserve!

"Mr. Chairman, I hate to correct you, but I was there running a bank during that crisis and it was not deposit insurance, but the price of a barrel of oil falling from $32 on Jan. 1 to $8 by February of 1986 that caused most banks of any size to run into trouble," I said. "I'm also sure that you remember the oil shock of 1973-74 when you were the part of the Ford administration. After that, the government encouraged the people in the oil business in both Texas and Louisiana to drill, and the statements by both Ford and Carter that they would protect the national oil industry and urged the industry to do more drilling. Then the government pulled the rug out from under the oil industry and in 1986 adopted the Reagan Tax Act that killed real estate development."

Greenspan didn't look real happy to be corrected by someone of my lowly pedigree. He looked at me over the top of his glasses and said, "My expert economists would disagree with your assumptions."

I was getting riled now and didn't need to hear about his so-called experts. "Expert economists remind me of the sports show hosts who can always tell you how they would have played the game but weren't on the field," I said. "Mr. Greenspan, I was there in the middle of it when seven out of nine banks in my home town of Lafayette, La., failed and not one of them was due to deposit insurance."

My fellow bankers had recovered their wits by then and quickly moved on to another topic before thanking the chairman for his time and hustling me out of his office.

You already know from my take on Sandy Weill, that the wily banker enlisted Greenspan's enthusiastic help to get Glass-Steagall repealed so that the merger between Weill's Travelers Co. and Citicorp would become legal two years after it was completed. But even before he and Citicorp CEO John Reed went to Washington to tell Greenspan about their merger plan, Weill was pretty sure Greenspan would help him.

Turns out, Weill had already tested Greenspan's support. Before doing the Citicorp deal, Weill had held merger talks with J.P. Morgan, the highly-respected bank that catered to wealthy individuals and corporations. J.P. Morgan's chairman Douglas "Sandy" Warner had dismissed Weill's overture immediately because Warner knew that the merger of an insurance company that owned a brokerage firm with a commercial bank was illegal under Glass-Steagall. But Weill trumped Warner's concerns by calling Greenspan to tell him what he was thinking about. Without even giving it much thought, Greenspan assured Weill that he was "open to the logic" of the merger. Ultimately Warner and Weill's own board of directors rejected the idea of merging Travelers with J.P. Morgan, but Greenspan was ready to back such a merger and was doubtless pleased when Weill brought him the Citicorp deal, mostly because Citicorp was a big bank that appeared to be in good financial shape. Appearances, of course, can be deceptive, as we have all discovered.

The second area in which I believe Greenspan failed to fulfill his duties to the nation was allowing two huge bubbles to form during his tenure without doing anything to prevent them and, in fact, encouraging the housing bubble. The first serious bubble was the crazed run-up in tech stocks late in the 1990s. In that case Greenspan said one thing, but did another. As tech stock prices soared to the sky and any startup with dot-com in its name could raise hundreds of millions in new stock offerings, Greenspan did note that there appeared to be some "irrational exuberance" surrounding the stock market.

Admittedly that remark caused a stir, but the stock market quickly shook off the implied warning and continued climbing. There's an old saying that the job of the Federal Reserve is to take away the punch bowl just when the party starts to get fun. It means that when the economy or the markets are exhibiting "irrational exuberance" it is the Fed's job to calm things down, either through jawboning or by actually raising interest rates to quench the exuberance. Although the Fed did raise interest rates in 1999 and 2000, the increase was not nearly sufficient to return sanity to the stock market, which kept climbing until it simply couldn't keep going. Once the selling started, it rapidly picked up speed and pretty soon it was all over. Individual investors who had poured everything they had into tech stocks lost billions of dollars as values collapsed. Ironically, it was the collapse of the tech stocks that then set us up for the subsequent housing bubble. Investors who had been burned by the stock market swore off investing in stocks and turned instead to real estate. And who was there to help them inflate that bubble? Alan Greenspan.

In the wake of the tech stock debacle the Federal Reserve again lowered interest rates to get the economy back on its feet. Those lower rates encouraged people to buy homes, to refinance their existing mortgages, and to buy houses and condos as investments. Like any bubble, the housing bubble started slowly, but steadily gained momentum, fueled by all kinds of creative mortgages that let people who could never have afforded a house under the old rules buy houses. Other homeowners kept refinancing their mortgages with bigger and bigger loans, effectively using the equity in their homes as piggy banks to fund massive spending. The banks and mortgage companies were having a great time. They would make these crazy loans and would then package those mortgages as securities and sell them to big investors so that they could then make even more mortgage loans. While rates stayed low and property values rose, more people began speculating on real estate, especially in such hot markets as Florida, California, and Arizona.

It was pretty obvious to me that we were heading for trouble and I certainly wasn't alone in that view: As early as 2001, Federal Reserve Governor Edward Gramlich warned that subprime mortgages could become a big problem. And in 2003, a staff economist warned Richard Syron, then the chief executive officer of Freddie Mac, that the risky loans it was making "would likely pose an enormous financial and reputational risk to the company and the country."

So what did the eminent economist at the head of the Fed think about the housing market? In 2005, when the bubble was growing faster and faster, Greenspan admitted that there was "a little froth" in the housing market. But he wasn't worried, he said, because the froth mostly amounted to local bubbles in a few markets. In my humble opinion, the person who has the responsibility for the nation's economic health ought to be able to see a bubble when it's right in front of him. Of course, the froth that Greenspan saw in 2005 came crashing down just two years later and he finally admitted that his use of the term "froth" was a euphemism for "bubble."

Many people don't realize that Greenspan doesn't have a very good record of spotting trouble. In 1985, for example, he was hired to review the financial health of Lincoln Savings & Loan, which had been taken over by Charles Keating, the head of a big construction firm. He gave the company a clean bill of health and sent a letter to the Federal Home Loan Bank of San Francisco supporting Keating's application for an exemption for Lincoln to a bank board rule forbidding substantial amounts of some investments. Of course, Lincoln went belly up in 1989, costing the federal government over $3 billion and leaving some 23,000 customers with worthless bonds. Keating pleaded guilty to fraud charges and spent more than four years in prison. When the "Keating Five" — a group of senators whose interference in a federal investigation of Lincoln brought them notoriety — were trying to explain their involvement in Lincoln and Keating's campaign contributions to them, they said they relied on Greenspan's report. All Greenspan could say was that he was wrong on Keating and did not think Keating would leverage his company that much or break the law.

There seems to be a pattern in the way Greenspan overlooks problems and then explains how he didn't think somebody would do something bad. That is especially true of his third major failure in not understanding the risks of the burgeoning derivatives market and seeking to regulate it. That, more than anything else, has been responsible for the crisis that almost wrecked the global financial system. Again, red flags were spotted, and not just by me: Felix Rohatyn, the investment banker who helped prevent New York City's bankruptcy in the 1970s when it suffered a financial crisis, called derivatives a "hydrogen bomb," and a few years ago Warren Buffett called them "financial weapons of mass destruction, carrying dangers that, while now latent, are potentially lethal." As early as 1994 the head of the government's General Accounting Office warned that the sudden failure of any of the big U.S. financial institutions trading in derivatives could "pose risks to others, including federally insured banks and the financial system as a whole." Pretty stunning, isn't it? Would you want your financial system exposed to such risks? Of course not.

So what did the Chairman of the Federal Reserve think about derivatives? Back in 2003 he told the Senate Banking Committee that "we think it would be a mistake" to regulate the derivatives market. "What we have found over the years in the marketplace is that derivatives have been an extraordinarily useful vehicle to transfer risk from those who shouldn't be taking it to those who are willing to and are capable of doing so." You mean, Mr. Chairman, companies like Bear Stearns? Lehman Brothers? AIG? Citigroup? Merrill Lynch? Bank of America?

Oops.

And it isn't like Greenspan hadn't experienced the kinds of problems derivatives could cause. In 1998 Long Term Capital Management, a hedge fund that included two Nobel laureates among its leadership, nearly collapsed as a result of derivative trades gone sour. It was Greenspan's Fed that had to rescue the firm and prop up the financial system to keep panic from spreading. Yet he continued to ignore the obvious risks.

Now that he's stepped down and his failures have become obvious to the world, all we've heard from the former chairman is that he "misread" the markets and is disappointed that his big bank buddies could be so greedy and irresponsible. He told a Congressional committee in October 2008: "Those of us who looked to the self-interest of lending institutions to protect shareholder's equity, myself especially, are in a state of shocked disbelief."

No apology. No admission of error. No acceptance of responsibility.

Thank God he's gone.

Chapter Twelve

THE TEXAN WHO KNEW IT ALL

There's one more person I want to see inducted into the Hall of Shame for bringing the world financial system to its knees: Phil Gramm. You might be surprised that someone like me from the Oil Patch would criticize a senior senator for the great state of Texas, but I can tell you that like so many others elected or appointed to high office, Phil Gramm lost his bearings and became part of the "in" crowd in Washington. Once he got submerged into the power games on Capitol Hill, he became a Texan in name only.

If Alan Greenspan is the god of free markets, Phil Gramm was his chief apostle. From his powerful post as chairman of the Senate Banking Committee Gramm preached his gospel of deregulation loudly and at length. He used his doctorate in economics to try to lord over other legislators who weren't so eminently qualified — as least to Gramm — to guide the nation's financial system toward freedom from government interference. It shouldn't come as a surprise that the big banks loved Phil Gramm. From 1989 to 2002, he was at the top of the charts among recipients of contributions from the financial industry.

Gramm did his worst work when Sandy Weill cooked up his scheme to merge Travelers and Citicorp. Of course, Alan Greenspan could have stopped that plan in its tracks had he just told Weill the merger would be against the law. But Greenspan saw the chance to undo some regulations, one of his favorite pastimes, and gave Weill two years to get Glass-Steagall repealed. In effect, Greenspan was giving his nod to Phil Gramm to seize the opportunity they both had been looking for to dispose of Glass-Steagall. Never one to turn down the chance to get credit for something, Gramm got together with Rep. Jim Leach of Iowa, head of the House Banking Committee; and Rep. Thomas J. Bliley Jr. of Virginia to introduce the Gramm-Leach-Bliley Bill, a measure that would knock down all the important barriers that kept risky investment firms from allying themselves with big, supposedly conservative, banks.

It didn't take a genius to see what would happen if Gramm-Leach-Bliley passed: It would turn over the core of our nation's financial system to gigantic firms that would be in the business of taking risks. Worse yet, the bill would split up regulation of the big firms, with the SEC watching over the brokerage arms of the companies while bank regulators would be in charge of the banking arms of the combined companies. Trouble was, there wasn't anyone watching over the entire industry.

Many of us in the community banking industry lobbied hard to prevent Gramm-Leach-Bliley from passing. I concentrated on Rep. Richard Baker of Louisiana, who assured me that Gramm-Leach-Bliley wasn't going to be that bad for community banks. It wasn't the community banks I was worried about, I told him, it was the future of our country. But they just wouldn't listen. Gramm pushed the bill through Congress by arguing that the nation needed to modernize its laws so that it could compete with the rest of the world. Frankly, I thought MidSouth Bank was doing a damn good job competing without the help of Phil Gramm!

But repealing Glass-Steagall wasn't Gramm's only "accomplishment." A year after he won that battle he went into overdrive to prevent any regulation of the growing market for derivatives like credit default swaps and collateralized debt obligations. Ironically, he was following up on work that his wife, Wendy, had done years earlier when she was heading up the Commodity Futures Trading Commission, which was supposed to oversee derivatives. She effectively exempted a lot of derivatives trades from supervision, and now her husband wanted to drive a stake through the heart of any thoughts of regulating them as the market for them swelled and some people began to sense danger. When the Commodity Futures Modernization Act that exempted derivatives from government oversight passed in December 2000, Gramm crowed that, "It will keep our markets modern, efficient, and innovative, and it guarantees that the United States will maintain its global dominance of financial markets."

The derivatives that Gramm protected were a result of the widespread push among banks and mortgage brokers to lure people into taking on mortgages they couldn't afford. These subprime loans were beginning to be seen as another source of danger as millions of people who otherwise would have been unable used the loans to buy houses, driving up the price of housing to astronomical heights in some communities. But with his doctorate in economics, Gramm didn't see any problem.

"Some people look at subprime lending and see evil," he said during a hearing over a proposal to curb so-called predatory lending. "I look at subprime lending and I see the American Dream in action." He cited his mother as an example: Years earlier she had gone to a finance company for a high-priced loan to buy a small house, becoming the first person in her family ever to own a home.

For Gramm, there was no such thing as a "predatory lender." There were only "predatory borrowers," people who knew they couldn't afford to make the payments on a mortgage, but took it anyway, prepared to walk away from the house when the payments became too much of a burden. He had a pretty low opinion of those kinds of people, never mind the fact that the loan documents were so complex most lawyers couldn't decipher them. But Gramm's view of predatory borrowers squared with some of his other pronouncements, such as his suggestion that food stamps be cut because "all our poor people are fat." Perhaps his most memorable line came during the 2008 presidential campaign when he was hoping that Sen. John McCain would name him Secretary of the Treasury if he were elected. Even as the worst economic crisis since the Great Depression was spreading across the United States, Gramm insisted that there wasn't any real problem and that America had become "a nation of whiners." So much for the value of a doctorate in economics!

As you might expect of a free-market guy like Gramm, he had lots of friends in business. Does it surprise you that his wife, Wendy, the one who deregulated derivatives as head of the Commodity Futures Trading Commission, later went on to become a board member at Enron? Seems like she would have been in an ideal position to detect the massive fraud that Enron was committing, but apparently she just didn't notice. And when it came time for Gramm to retire from the U.S. Senate, it just seemed entirely appropriate that he should take up a post as the vice chairman of UBS, the giant Swiss bank. From that post he successfully lobbied to block efforts to curb predatory lending.

I suppose there is a little justice in the world. As a result of its heavy trading in the credit default swaps that Phil and Wendy Gramm made sure would not be regulated, UBS posted billions of dollars of losses in 2008 and had to be bailed out by the Swiss government to the tune of $60 billion. I don't remember Phil Gramm speaking out against that interference by government.

PART IV
Endgame

Chapter Thirteen

A Good Crisis Going to Waste

I can't tell you how frustrating it is to have spent more than twenty years watching the American banking system becoming bigger and riskier and not being able to do anything about it. As you now know, I warned lots of people lots of times, but for whatever reason I failed to convince the powers that be to do anything to stop our headlong slide into disaster. Even more frustrating was the fact that when some of these crises first arose, I became convinced that we as a nation, through Congress, the administration that was in power, and the regulators who were watching over the industry, were going to do the right thing and fix the problems. Each time I was disappointed.

Regretfully, that same thing is happening once again as we make our way through the "rescue" plan that the Bush and Obama administrations have promised will fix the problem. There's already plenty of evidence that there will be no real fix and that we might very well be making things worse instead of better. Of course, what we call the rescue plan isn't a single plan at all; it has been from the outset a makeshift and often haphazard response to a crisis that occurred on an unimaginable scale and with unprecedented speed. It would hardly be fair for me or anyone else to assume that when hit with these huge problems, any single person or institution could have gotten everything right the first time. Nevertheless, I would have hoped that as we began to move back from the edge of a cataclysmic failure of the global financial system, and as the pressures to do anything and everything to save the system eased that we would have become more thoughtful and reflective, thinking more about what went wrong and how to head off a recurrence in the future. Instead, it seems more likely that we have simply uttered a huge sigh of relief — and then went back to business as usual.

If there is one point that I have tried to hammer home in this book, it is that "too big to fail" is an unworkable doctrine for the regulation of a sound financial system. We simply cannot allow financial institutions to become too big to fail. That is precisely what put us in the fix we're in today. And at first, as the government struggled to find a way to save the financial system, it seemed yet again as if we were finally going to do the right thing. I was gratified when I first heard about the government's plan to rescue the financial system through the purchase, with taxpayer money, of the toxic assets that the big banks held. Was I happy to be spending taxpayer money buying those assets? Not at all. But I envisioned the Troubled Asset Relief Program of 2008 as a necessary first step to beginning the orderly breakup of the huge banks and other financial firms that created the problems. There was lots of talk in Congressional testimony (including mine) and in news conferences and interviews about the fatal flaws in a system that allowed financial firms to become too big to fail. The obvious solution was to be sure no institution became that big. In my own vision of the future, I figured that soon, perhaps within five years or so, we would have restored our banking system to the point where we would all have confidence in the banks and their regulators. Smaller would be better!

Alas, I was destined once again to be disappointed. What has happened is exactly the opposite of what I hoped to see. The big banks have not been broken up and made smaller. Instead they've been merged or bought and are today bigger than they were before the crisis began. Taken together, the big banks now represent an even bigger part of the financial industry than they did before. Just consider: Bank of America now owns Merrill Lynch and Countrywide, JPMorganChase has absorbed Bear Stearns and Washington Mutual, and Wells Fargo has acquired Wachovia. The Treasury and the Federal Reserve have actually blessed and even forced some of those mergers rather than opposing them as the unacceptable continuation of a dangerous trend that nearly destroyed us. And if that isn't bad enough, the Federal Reserve is handing out bank charters willy-nilly to entities that don't even look like a bank. Today, Goldman Sachs, General Motors Acceptance Corp., and General Electric Credit Corp. are all banks. Making big banks bigger and giving banking charters to companies that aren't banks is not the solution to our problems!

There is plenty of evidence, too, that the people we trust to understand these things don't really comprehend them even as their arrogance remains unabated. I still shake my head in wonderment at Treasury Secretary Henry Paulsen's naked grab for power when the crisis first broke. His original "rescue plan" was a three-page bill that he wanted Congress to pass almost instantly that would have given him unprecedented power to bail out big banks and brokerages, with whom he had very close relations as the former head of Goldman Sachs, with almost no accountability to Congress or anyone else. Congress has made some mistakes over the years that contributed to our problems, but it wasn't going to just roll over and play dead. Paulsen was sent back to draft a more explicit plan, which he did with the help of Ben Bernanke, chairman of the Federal Reserve, and Timothy Geithner, president of the New York Federal Reserve Bank. That plan was the Troubled Asset Repurchase Program that I so fervently hoped would be the first step in breaking down the big banks. But what I didn't know and, more worrisome, what Paulsen, Bernanke, and Geithner didn't know, was that they simply didn't have enough resources to pull it off. They couldn't begin to buy up enough toxic assets to save the big banks.

During the presidential campaign, Barack Obama promised he would bring change to Washington. That would be good if it were true. But when I look at what he's done about the financial crisis I don't see that much has changed. Larry Summers, who under President Clinton helped set us on the road to ruin, is now top economic adviser to Obama. Geithner, who as head of the New York Federal Reserve regulated the big banks that got us into trouble, has replaced Paulsen as Treasury Secretary. What's really changed except the names on the door? Nothing. It's like Louisiana State University is playing the University of Florida and LSU picks a fan out of the stands to be the referee. UF objects, so LSU just picks another fan. I know that the Democrats instead of the Republicans now head the important banking and finance committees in Congress, but they're listening to the same old advice from the same old lobbyists for the big banks that have been appearing before them for years.

The bad practices and the arrogance of the big banks and Wall Street firms continue unabated as well. "Arrogant" is the only way to describe companies like AIG that took huge sums of taxpayer money and then paid it out as fat bonuses to the executives and traders who created the problems that required us to bail them out. And how is it that if we should be paying bonuses to financial executives for long-term performance, the bankers at Goldman Sachs got huge bonuses in the second quarter of 2009 even as the crisis continued and the rest of the country struggled with unemployment nearing 10 percent?

I thought Rahm Emanuel, the former Democratic congressman from Chicago and now Obama's chief of staff, said something smart when he was asked why he was taking the staff job in the face of so many overwhelming problems confronting the new administration. Never one to back down from a challenge, Emanuel just smiled and said, "A crisis is a terrible thing to waste."

I'm afraid we're wasting this one.

Chapter Fourteen

WHERE DO WE GO NOW?

The worst of the financial crisis that began in 2008 probably is behind us, although I'm not so naïve as to guarantee that. But if that's true, the real question now is what the future holds. Will we slip back into our old ways of doing business, giving the powerful even more power and allowing greed and ego to run rampant on Wall Street and in Washington? Or will we really change our ways and reshape our financial and governmental institutions to serve their real purpose, which is providing capital so that the rest of us can go about getting our jobs done, creating products, services and jobs and making the world a better place?

As I suggested in the last chapter, I'm not hopeful. It is often exceedingly difficult for people to admit they have made mistakes. There is no doubt in my mind that people like Alan Greenspan, Sandy Weill, Hugh McColl, and Phil Gramm bear some responsibility for the financial trauma we have suffered for the past two years. The toll has been staggering in terms of lost jobs, homes, and savings. Yet from none of those powerful people who helped cause these losses have we heard the first indications of regret or apology. It is like they are living in another world and, the truth is, with their wealth they probably are in a different world from the rest of us.

But without admitting mistakes, we can do little to remedy them. And that's what worries me most. Too many people who were involved in creating the crisis are involved in solving it: Timothy Geithner, Larry Summers, et al. Sure, a few senior financial executives deservedly lost their jobs (although most took home some huge severance checks), but far too few to drive home the point that we desperately need fundamental change.

As I noted, the big banks are bigger, at least relatively speaking, than they were before the crisis. Before the meltdown, only Fannie Mae and Freddie Mac had the implicit backing of the U.S. Treasury. Now a dozen banks and even some big companies that aren't even banks have that backing. That's hardly progress toward solving our problems.

Perhaps I'm being too idealistic in thinking that we can recapture a time when banking was a respected profession and the local banker played the role of financing the economic activities of his or her community. Nevertheless, I firmly believe there are some steps we can take to restore credibility to our financial system and avoid the risk of future crises like this one. To that end I offer here 20 specific recommendations, along with my reasoning, that, if adopted, would go a long way toward creating that future.

1. Restore the separation of commercial banks and investments banks. Unlike current Congress members, their predecessors who endured The Great Depression didn't let a good crisis go to waste. They passed the Glass-Steagall Act because they understood the huge temptation that arose when commercial banks could risk their depositors' money on speculative ventures. Sadly, we forgot that wisdom and replaced Glass-Steagall with the Gramm-Leach-Bliley Act. Now it's time to do the right thing and repeal that misguided piece of legislation and replace it with essentially the same language contained in the original Glass-Steagall Act. Greed is a powerful force among financiers, and we have a responsibility to be sure we hold it in check by law.

2. Define the term "bank" very specifically and very conservatively. To me, a company that purports to be a bank must get at least half of its business from taking deposits and making loans in the markets the bank serves. A company that merely issues credit cards or that serves as the internal funding source for a commercial company like General Motors is in no way, shape, or form a bank and should not be allowed to act under the guise of being a bank.

3. Never allow a financial firm to become "too big to fail." I understand that in some cases the term "too big to fail" is a political concept, not an economic one, but we need to put some economic limits on financial firms. I believe that any financial firm that amasses assets of more than $500 billion will possess the clout to severely damage our economy in the event it fails. Therefore, we need to require any financial firm with assets in excess of $500 billion to begin now to divest itself of some of those in order to reach a level of $500 billion or less within three years. Thereafter, the cap of $500 billion should be adjusted to every five years to reflect the effects of inflation.

4. Make shareholders take a real risk when they invest in a financial company. Looking forward, any financial institution that requires a government bailout will be liquidated over a period of five years with no recourse, and stockholders will receive nothing for their shares. It should anger every taxpayer that the government used your money to bail out not just the corporate entities that were Citigroup and Bank of America, but also the investors who should have been at risk for the failure of the managements those shareholders elected.

5. Put the proper onus of responsibility on the chief executive officer. The CEO of any bank that requests government assistance shall tender his resignation to the government upon making that request. The government has the option to accept or reject that resignation as it sees fit upon review of the bank's condition.

6. Focus regulatory power on the riskiest entities. "One-size-fits-all" regulation is no longer appropriate for a financial system that ranges in size from giant national banks to tiny community banks. The failure of a local bank with $100 million in assets poses no threat to the national or international financial system and consequently needs a level of regulation aimed only at protecting depositors. The largest 25 banks, even after being scaled back to the point of no longer being "too big to fail," nevertheless might pose a systemic risk if one or more should fail. Therefore regulators should devote much more time, attention and manpower to monitoring and correcting deficiencies in the operations of those banks.

7. Provide regular reports on the condition of large banks. The regulators in the previous recommendation who are devoting more attention and manpower to monitoring and correcting deficiencies in the operations of the big banks should make annual reports to Congress on the health of those banks, the risks they have assumed, and what actions have been and will be taken to contain those risks.

8. Require boards of directors to own a substantial stake in banks they govern. Directors of public companies have not always been deeply involved in the operations of those companies. If they were required to a have a substantial portion of their net worth invested in the company they oversee — some "skin in the game," so to speak — they would doubtless be much more interested in looking closely at how management is doing its job. A "substantial portion of their net worth" would, of course, be different for board members who are not widely regarded as wealthy, such as academics, heads of charitable organizations, or others whose guidance is valued.

9. Realign the SEC to focus on companies that pose the most risk. In the aftermath of the Enron and WorldCom scandals, Congress adopted the Sarbanes-Oxley Act, which imposed huge accounting and verification responsibilities on public companies regardless of their size. The requirements are an enormous burden on small companies that pose little or no risk and should be removed. Only large companies whose failure would harm a large number of investors should be required to meet the Sarbanes-Oxley requirements.

10. Revamp membership of the Federal Reserve's

Advisory Council. Currently, this secretive organization is made up solely of representatives of the biggest banks. Small and medium-sized banks, defined as those with assets of less than $1 billion and $10 billion, respectively, should each have representation equal to that of the largest banks.

11. Stop the flow of powerful legislators into the lobbying firms that represent big banks. The lawmakers who serve on such powerful committees as the Senate Banking Committee and the House Banking Committee, as well as senior regulators, know that if they accommodate the wishes of the big banks they will have lucrative jobs waiting for them as lobbyists when they leave Congress. Phil Gramm, the former Texas Senator, who is a highly paid UBS executive, is a prime example. Much of that conflict of interest would be eliminated if financial firms were prohibited from paying any former legislator or regulator an annual salary in excess of that paid to the president of the United States.

12. Restrict bank spending on lobbying. The playing field needs to be level, therefore no bank can spend more than $250,000 in any year, directly or indirectly, to lobby Congress or regulators.

13. Broaden the expertise on the Federal Reserve Board and the Federal Open Market Committee. Recognize that experience can be obtained from men and women who have held leadership roles in smaller financial institutions. Require the president of the New York Federal Reserve Bank, who serves as the vice chairman of the FOMC, be subject to Senate approval.

14. Impose term limits on the Chairman of the Federal Reserve Board. Alan Greenspan served — I should say "ruled" — as chairman of the Fed for 19 years through the terms of four presidents. That's simply too long. The Fed chairman should be limited to two four-year terms.

15. Ban issuance of bank charters for Industrial Loan Companies. These entities act as banks but are not regulated as banks. There is no reason to mix banking and standard commercial transactions.

16. Restrict real estate mortgages to 80 percent of the value of the home. Just as directors of banks should have some "skin in the game," so, too, should homeowners. Without that equity stake it is simply too easy for a homeowner to walk away from a mortgage.

17. Regulate swaps and other derivatives. These are the toxic assets that underlay the near-collapse of the global financial system. Their values must be transparent and the extent of their trading must be regulated.

18. Regulate consumer lending. Credit has a proper place in a modern economy, but predatory lending does not. Excessive credit card fees, payday loans, and other means of misleading consumers must be restricted. There is plenty of profit to be made without taking advantage of unsophisticated consumers.

19. Bring the "real world" to Washington. Too often insiders and the powerful constitute the governing membership of federal agencies and boards. It is crucial that those agencies and boards require that some portion of the governing structure be composed of ordinary citizens and businesspeople.

20. End secrecy in government. While the needs of national security must be taken into account, there is too much secrecy in government proceedings. Absent a compelling national security rationale, most meetings of governmental agencies and Congressional committees should be open to the public, and hearings should be conducted if at all possible outside of Washington, D.C., and rotated among various cities.

Will these recommendations, if adopted, solve all the problems we face today?

Probably not. But I know that if we don't undertake fundamental changes in the financial system, the dangers that caught up with us in 2008 will continue to exist and will, inevitably, catch up with us again. We may not be so lucky next time. The "best and brightest" in Washington and on Wall Street kept saying "Trust us, we know what we are doing." We did trust them, but they didn't know what they were doing. Through greed, ego, and incompetence they have done untold damage to our economy. I'm not thinking of myself when I make these recommendations. I've had a long and fruitful career despite all these problems. Rather, I'm thinking about the shape of the future that my children and grandchildren will inherit. I want them to live the American dream just as I have. But the people and policies that created the current mess could very well create another one that steals away that future from my children and grandchildren. I know that as a banker I run a certain risk in writing this book that is critical of very powerful people and institutions. But I could not stand idly by and watch my country continue down the path it was on. I hope you agree that we, the common people, need to reassert our authority and interest in having a well-regulated financial system for the sake of our heirs. Thank you for your valuable time and attention in reading these humble words from a small-town community banker who has had a front-row seat in the events that led to the financial crisis of 2008.

God bless and save America!

Acknowledgments

This book would never have come about were it not for the encouragement of my fellow bankers in America, especially Dale Leighty of Colorado, David Hayes of Tennessee, and Terry Jorde of North Dakota. I also owe a debt of gratitude to Ken Gunther and Camden Fine of Independent Community Bankers of America for giving me the opportunity to serve the banking industry at the national level. The board of directors of MidSouth Bank has been gracious about allowing me to spend the last 10 years of my career traveling the country to serve the industry I love. And I could not have done that traveling without the dedicated support of my banking team at MidSouth Bank in Lafayette, who live their commitments to their communities.

I have benefited immensely from the encouragement and hard work of friends more knowledgeable about publishing who graciously volunteered their time and expertise. Steve May, Leslie Turk, and Odie Terry did yeoman duty in reading and critiquing my words and paving the way for getting the book from computer screen to bound pages. Doug Sease brought his experience in producing a number of books to the editing process and Ken Wells has my deep appreciation for putting me together with Doug. My wife, Brenda, devoted untold hours to reworking my words and compiling the original manuscript. When it all seemed too daunting, her words of encouragement renewed my energy. Sally Gary, Shaleen Pellerin, Hannah

Kossover, and Mattie Cook at MidSouth Bank kept track of my many random notes, e-mails, and musings to be sure that I didn't lose something amid the mass of papers and messages. Finally, I owe a huge debt of gratitude to all my fellow community bankers who have given me their support over the years and who have never given up hope of restoring the banking industry to its rightful place serving the American people.

Appendix I

*The principles of sound banking aren't difficult to understand
— and they certainly aren't new. The following excerpt is from
a letter to bankers written in 1863 by Hugh McCulloch, the
Comptroller of the Currency. If only we hadn't strayed from his
very practical advice!*

Let no loans be made that are not secured beyond a reasonable contingency. Do nothing to foster and encourage speculation. Give facilities only to legitimate and prudent transactions. Make your discounts on as short time as the business of your customers will permit, and insist upon the payment of all paper at maturity, no matter whether you need the money or not. Never renew a note or bill merely because you may not know where to place the money with equal advantage if the paper is paid. In no other way can you properly control your discount line, or make it at all times reliable.

Distribute your loans rather than concentrate them in a few hands. Large loans to a single individual or firm, although sometimes proper and necessary, are generally injudicious, and frequently unsafe. Large borrowers are apt to control the bank; and when this is the relation between a bank and its customers, it is not difficult to decide which in the end will suffer. Every dollar that a bank loans above its capital and surplus it owes for, and its managers are therefore under the strongest obligations to its creditors, as well as to its stockholders, to keep its discounts constantly under its control.

Treat your customer liberally, bearing in mind the fact that a bank prospers as its customers prosper, but never permit them to dictate your policy.

If you doubt the propriety of discounting an offering, give the bank the benefit of the doubt and decline it; never make a discount if you doubt the propriety of doing it. If you have reason to distrust the integrity of a customer, close his account. Never deal with a rascal under the impression that you can prevent him from cheating you. The risk in such cases is greater than the profits.

Pay your officers such salaries as will enable them to live comfortably and respectably without stealing; and require of them their entire services. If an officer lives beyond his income, dismiss him; even if his excess of expenditures can be explained consistently with his integrity, still dismiss him. Extravagance, if not a crime, very naturally leads to crime. A man cannot be a safe officer of a bank who spends more than he earns.

The capital of a bank should be reality, not a fiction; and it should be owned by those who have money to lend, and not by borrowers. The Comptroller will endeavor to prevent, by all means within his control, the creation of a nominal capital by national banks, by the use of their circulation, or any other artificial means, and in his efforts to do this, he confidently expects the co-operation of all the well-managed banks.

Pursue a straightforward, upright, legitimate banking business. Never be tempted by the prospect of large returns to do anything but what may be properly done under the National Currency Act. 'Splendid financiering' is not legitimate banking, and 'splendid financiers' in banking are generally either humbugs or rascals.

Appendix II

Do your total assets exceed one-fourth of the 2009 federal deficit?

Do you fund a significant portion of your balance sheet with non-domestic deposits?

Was your CEO's 2008 compensation dramatically reduced, yet still exceeded the gross domestic product of Ghana?

Have you received major capital infusions from taxpayers or FDIC asset and debt guarantees, yet maintain that you are independent and solvent?

Do you argue with auditors as to whether or not you should bring significant amounts of assets "back onto your balance sheet?"

Is your bank systemically important?

Lest my account of the circumstances that got us into such deep trouble has you feeling a bit gloomy about the future, I thought it might be good to end with a dash of whimsy (which isn't as whimsical as you might think), courtesy of a friend in the banking industry.

NO →

Sorry. You are not systemically important. You will be allowed to fail.

 **YES** →

Congratulations! You are systemically important. You will be endlessly propped up and can do as you please.

Index